THE GOLDEN RULES OF POSITIVE
PUPPY TRAINING

The Golden Rules of Positive Puppy Training

CompanionHouse Books™ is an imprint of Fox Chapel Publishers International Ltd.

Project Team
Editor: Amy Deputato
Copy Editor: Colleen Dorsey
Design: Mary Ann Kahn
Translator: Ulatus

Originally published in French as *Tout se joue avant 1 an!* Copyright © 2018 Larousse
Project Team (French edition)
Publication Management: Isabelle Jeuge-Maynart and Ghislaine Stora
Editorial Management: Catherine Delprat
Editing: Edi+ and Liza Person-Lisiecki
Proofreading: Laurence Alvado
Graphic Design and Page Layout: Emmanuel Chaspoul
Cover: Aurore Elie
Production: Donia Faiz

ISBN 978-1-62187-187-3

The Cataloging-in-Publication Data is on file with the Library of Congress.

This book has been published with the intent to provide accurate and authoritative information in regard to the subject matter within. While every precaution has been taken in the preparation of this book, the author and publisher expressly disclaim any responsibility for any errors, omissions, or adverse effects arising from the use or application of the information contained herein. The techniques and suggestions are used at the reader's discretion and are not to be considered a substitute for veterinary care. If you suspect a medical problem, consult your veterinarian.

Fox Chapel Publishing
903 Square Street
Mount Joy, PA 17552

Fox Chapel Publishers International Ltd.
7 Danefield Road, Selsey (Chichester)
West Sussex PO20 9DA, U.K.

www.facebook.com/companionhousebooks

We are always looking for talented authors. To submit an idea, please send a brief inquiry to acquisitions@foxchapelpublishing.com.

Printed and bound in Singapore
23 22 21 20   2 4 6 8 10 9 7 5 3 1

THE GOLDEN RULES OF POSITIVE
PUPPY TRAINING

Everything You Need to Know for Your Puppy's First Year

Dr. Jean Cuvelier

Illustrations by Jean-Yves Grall

Contents

EASY   MEDIUM   DIFFICULT

Introduction 6

PART 1
WHO IS YOUR DOG? 9

An Opportunistic Wolf 10

A Unique Personality 14

The Breed Does Not Make the Dog 18

PART 2
WHAT MAKES A GOOD OWNER? 23

Be His Best Friend 24

Work on Improving Yourself 26

Demonstrate Empathy 28

Know How to Communicate 32

Give Clear Cues 34

Build a Relationship of Trust 38

Establish Clear and Fair Rules 40

Meet His Basic Needs 42

Provide for His Safety 46

Understand His Instincts 48

Provide Socialization and Recreation 49

Learn Canine Massage 50

Provide Physical Activity 52

Allow Him to Learn and Be Useful 54

Is Your Dog Happy? 56

PART 3
HOW TO TRAIN YOUR DOG 59

Mind Map: Positive Training 60

Choose a Dog-Friendly Training Method 62

Positive Reinforcement (Reward) 64

"Jackpots" and Secondary Rewards 68

Effects of Rewards 70

Positive Punishment 72

Effects of Positive Punishment 74

Negative Punishment 78

Negative Reinforcement 79

Reward versus Punishment:
Make the Right Choice 81

Learning through Observation 82

A Good Trainer's Equipment 84

PART 4
TRAINING TIMELINE 87

Mind Map: Training Timeline 88

From Birth to Two Months 90

From Two to Six Months 96

SOCIALIZATION 103

Perfect His Canine Communication Skills 104

Acclimate Him to His Environment 106

Introduce Him to People 110

Introduce Him to Other Animals 112

BASIC SKILLS **115**

🦴🦴 Independence 116

🦴🦴 House-Training 118

🦴 Coming When Called (Recall) 120

🦴 Going to His Bed and 🦴🦴 Staying There 121

🦴🦴 Enclosure Training............................ 124

🦴 Sit and Down 126

🦴🦴 Stay 130

🦴🦴 Eating Calmly 131

🦴🦴 Self-Control 133

🦴 The Collar, 🦴🦴 Muzzle and 🦴🦴 Harness....... 135

🦴🦴 Walking on Leash 136

🦴 Nail Clipping and Other Grooming 140

🦴 Visiting the Veterinarian 141

🦴 Riding in the Car 142

🦴🦴 Giving Up a Toy.............................. 143

🦴🦴🦴 Interrupting Behavior 144

🦴 Look at Me 145

ADVANCED CUES AND TRICKS **147**

From Six Months to One Year..................... 148

A Puppy's Daily Activities 150

🦴🦴🦴 Speak and Quiet 151

🦴🦴🦴 Leave It 152

🦴🦴🦴 Fetch...................................... 154

🦴🦴🦴 Closing a Door with His Nose 156

🦴🦴 Sit Pretty 157

🦴🦴 Play Dead 158

🦴🦴 High Five 159

A Good Trainer's Secrets......................... 160

PART 5
POSITIVE BEHAVIOR MODIFICATION **163**

Mind Map: Positive Behavior Modification 164

Maintain the Relationship 166

Analyze the Situation 167

Take Action.................................... 168

Consider Your Dog's Instincts and Emotions 172

BEHAVIOR MODIFICATION TECHNIQUES ... **179**

Desensitization................................. 180

Counterconditioning 183

Interruption and Redirection 187

Extinction..................................... 188

A Canine Role Model 190

How Long Does Behavorial Change Take? 191

Summary of Techniques......................... 192

When Should Medications Be Used? 194

APPENDIX **199**

Timeline of Puppy Milestones 200

Training Timeline............................... 202

GLOSSARY **204**

INDEX **206**

INTRODUCTION

FOR THE LOVE OF THE DOG, STOP PULLING ON THE LEASH!

In this book, I propose changing your perception of dogs and their training. A dog's first year is critical to his future development: with a loving mother, a competent breeder, a nurturing environment, a good owner, and positive training, your dog will become the perfect companion and will only bring you joy throughout his lifetime.

As Confucius says, "A picture is worth a thousand words." To improve clarity and make memorization easier, many infographics and illustrations have been included in this book to help you better understand how to train the wonderful gift of life you are responsible for.

A DOG IS A GIFT; DON'T FORGET TO UNTIE THE RIBBON!

WHY ARE THERE SO MANY ILLUSTRATIONS?

Images speed up memorization. The proof is in the pictures!

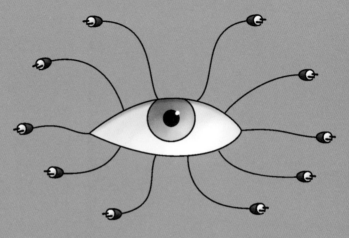

People follow instructions with images three times better than with text alone.

WE ARE VISUALLY WIRED

50% of our brain is involved in visual processing.

~ 70% of our sensory receptors are located in our eyes.

We understand the meaning of an image in less than 1/10 of a second.

10%

80%

20%

We remember 80% of what we see, 20% of what we read, and 10% of what we hear.

7

Part 1

Who Is Your Dog?

Adopting a puppy is a wonderful adventure, provided you really get to know this creature who will share your life for more than ten years. In order to make the right choice, you need to know how the bond between man and canine has developed over time, how a dog's personality is formed, and about the various breeds and their inherent skills.

An Opportunistic Wolf

Dogs have retained the memory of their distant ancestor, the wolf, in their genes. But after a very long common history and life shared with humans, the canine species has undergone physical changes and acquired new skills in order to integrate with their human families and become, so to speak, "children" of their families.

UNITED FOR BETTER LIVES

A Win-Win Relationship

About 25,000 years ago, the first wolf to approach human camps was a rather brave outsider who was attracted by food waste. He quickly understood all the benefits that entailed befriending the human species. It is in this way that we believe the wolf allowed itself to become domesticated. In return, the humans gained a guard, a hunter, and an efficient garbage collector. The first relationship between the dog's ancestor and humankind was thus established on a "win-win" premise.

An Emotional Bond

Due to constant contact, what was initially a purely utilitarian relationship gave way to a relationship of selfless trust. We can imagine that it all began with a hungry, orphaned wolf cub found refuge with a compassionate human family. The early contact with humans and the maternal care given to the cub made it possible to establish a mutual, lasting bond between the cub and his rescuers.

Even today, few humans can resist the irrepressible desire to take care of a puppy who noisily expresses his distress. The maternal instinct ingrained in the human brain and the puppy's expressive gaze have a lot to do with this instant connection.

Without the intervention of a good human soul, this little wolf cub would certainly have died. But instead of being solely a useful animal, he became what can be considered the promising beginnings of our pet dog. Today, while some breeds still play the double role of working dog and pet dog, many breeds are primarily companion animals.

MULTIPLE AND VARIED DESCENDANTS

Owing to the permanent presence of the dog among humans, we were able to start a process of selection that resulted in dogs who were adapted to the functions assigned to them: guarding, hunting, tracking, companionship, etc. Empirical at first, this selection improved over time and resulted in the creation of more than 300 canine breeds, each with distinct physical and behavioral characteristics.

Despite their differences, the Chihuahua, Shar-Pei, German Shepherd, Weimaraner, Afghan Hound, and Great Dane all have a common ancestor. If they wanted, they could mate and have viable offspring, which, if nothing else, would be original!

Through its contact with humans, the canine species has learned how to socialize better with us.

A DIFFERENT GENOME

Comparing the genomes of wolves and dogs, researchers have discovered that some genes involved in brain development and starch metabolism were modified during domestication. Thus, due to contact with humans, dog has lost his large head (30% less head volume than that of the wolf) and has gained a better ability to digest starch. Just look at the speed with which a dog goes for the leftover pasta!

AT HUMAN SCHOOL

The communication between dogs and their human companions is only slightly similar to the communication that dogs have among themselves. At human school, the dog, without losing his first language, perfected a second one. Over time, this hardworking student learned to communicate better with his teachers, and they have built a wonderful, unique relationship that is based on love, trust, and companionship.

Dogs have learned to read the emotions on human faces.

A study conducted by a team of researchers at the University of Veterinary Medicine in Vienna, Austria, shows that dogs can distinguish between happy and angry facial expressions.

Dogs have learned to decipher finger-pointing gestures.

An experiment conducted to compare the interspecific communication skills of dogs and wolves showed that dogs have greater ability to decipher finger-pointing than wolves do. This proves that the dog's ability was not inherited from his ancestor but rather was developed while evolving alongside humans.

In the experiment, a dog was given two opaque containers, an empty one and one with food inside it. A person pointing to the food container allowed the dog to find the food more quickly. Dogs trust humans to such an extent that if someone were to point to the wrong container, the dog would choose it—even though his strong sense of smell clearly tells him which container is the food container.

Dogs have learned to ask for help with their eyes.

When a dog is faced with an unsolvable problem—for example, not being able to reach his ball—research has shown that the dog seeks to establish eye contact with a human, as if to ask for help. In contrast, a wolf will instead look at the object of the problem.

Dogs have learned to recognize a human's attention.

A dog is sensitive to and aware of his owner's eyes and perceives them as an indication of where his owner's attention is focused. For example, if you give your dog the cue to lie down while looking at him, he is much more likely to respond correctly than if you are looking at your phone or facing another direction. This behavior is similar to that of a student who ignores the classroom rules when the teacher's back is turned.

Dogs have learned to recognize the emotions conveyed through voice inflections.

Thanks to magnetic resonance imaging (MRI), Hungarian researchers have proven that the brains of dogs and humans react in the same way to similar sounds, especially to emotionally charged sounds, such as crying or laughing. Both the dog and the human would have inherited this ability from their common ancestor, who is at least 100 million years old. This shows the richness of the interactions between humans and their dogs.

Dogs have learned to show their affection for humans just by looking at them.

Works published in the American journal *Science* show a rise in oxytocin (the hormone associated with love, trust, attachment, pleasure, and social connection) in the brains of dogs and their owners when they look into each other's eyes. However, this is not the case when the dog is replaced by a wolf, even one that is raised by humans. This confirms that the dog did not inherit this trait but developed it during domestication.

This kind of hormonal response also occurs between a mother and child. This explains why, when a woman looks into a puppy's eyes, she experiences the irresistible urge to take care of him. Dog owners often use the term "my baby" to refer to their dogs, and that finds its full meaning here. If your dog looks at you, it's not just because he wants a treat but because he loves you.

A Unique Personality

A dog's personality reflects the way he perceives and reacts to the environment. It mainly develops during the initial months of a dog's life; nevertheless, it can evolve throughout his life, depending on his experiences. Personality helps explain a dog's behavior. It depends on the dog's character traits.

CHARACTER TRAITS

Character traits result from both genes (innate) and environmental factors (acquired). According to some researchers, a dog has five primary character traits, all of which together form his personality.

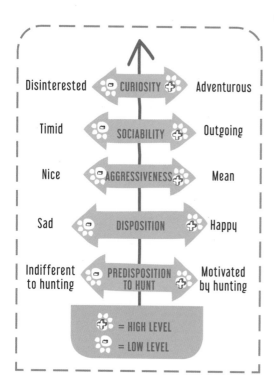

Disinterested	CURIOSITY	Adventurous
Timid	SOCIABILITY	Outgoing
Nice	AGGRESSIVENESS	Mean
Sad	DISPOSITION	Happy
Indifferent to hunting	PREDISPOSITION TO HUNT	Motivated by hunting

= HIGH LEVEL
= LOW LEVEL

A COMPLEX FORMULA

A dog's personality is like a pizza: the dough is the genes, and the toppings, the oven, the cooking time, and the temperature comprise the environmental factors. All pizzas have a common, similar base, yet each one is different.

Genetic Influence

At birth, a puppy has 39 pairs of chromosomes and approximately 20,000 genes; half of them are inherited

> Personality is the result of a subtle mixture of genes and environmental factors.

from his father and half from his mother. Some of these genes affect brain development, particularly the ability of neurons to interconnect. The impact of these genes on the dog's personality is undeniable; however, if a dog, even one born with an excellent learning capacity, lives in an environment with limited stimuli, he cannot achieve much.

Environmental Influence

A dog's brain is not completely developed at birth. It is made up of a set of poorly organized neurons. Stimuli from the environment cause the brain to organize itself into a network of functional neurons. The more numerous and positive the stimuli are, the more numerous and stable the connections (synapses) between neurons will be.

This cerebral plasticity allows the puppy to escape genetic determinism, as many personality traits are only expressed in the presence of certain environmental factors. Thus, two dogs with the same genotype may, depending on their individual histories, have two different personalities.

Training is essential for the puppy to stabilize neural connections among the set of possible connections provided by their genetic makeup.

> Genes are nothing more than a promise whose fulfillment depends on the environment.

The Brain-Development Timeline of a Puppy

When a dog becomes an adult, learning deficits are difficult, if not impossible, to overcome.

DEVELOPMENTAL TIMELINE OF A PUPPY'S BRAIN

Day 0–Day 15: Increase in the number of neurons

Day 15–Day 28: Increase in the number of connections (synapses)

Day 28–Month 3: Maturation and selection of connections (synapses)

Month 3–Puberty: Usage and stabilization of connections (synapses)

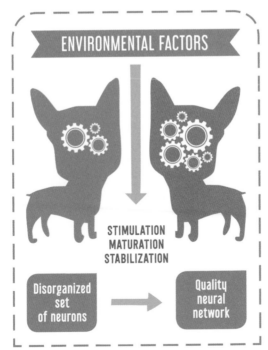

ENVIRONMENTAL FACTORS

STIMULATION
MATURATION
STABILIZATION

Disorganized set of neurons → Quality neural network

> At birth, a puppy is like a rough diamond whose eventual quality depends on his environment, and his owner is somewhat like a jeweler, helping the puppy fulfill his potential.

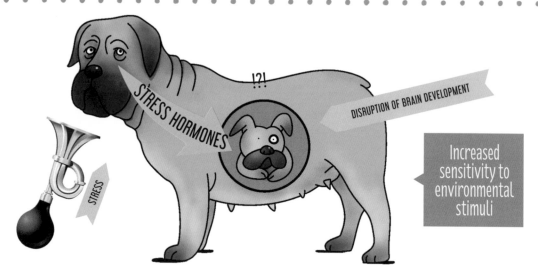

STRESS HORMONES

DISRUPTION OF BRAIN DEVELOPMENT

STRESS

Increased sensitivity to environmental stimuli

VARYING ENVIRONMENTAL FACTORS

An adult dog's emotional stability is largely influenced by the maternal environment in which the puppy lived.

Maternal Relationship

In his mother's womb, a puppy feels his mother's stress through hormones (e.g., cortisol, adrenaline). These hormones affect the brain's development and maturation and increase the puppy's sensitivity to subsequent environmental stimuli.

After the mother gives birth, an invisible bond is created between her and the puppies. The mother becomes a secure base from which the puppies can go out and explore the world. A calm, well-socialized mother will encourage her puppies to explore and give them self-confidence. Conversely, an anxious, poorly socialized mother will limit her puppies' exploration and increase their fear of the outside world.

The saying "like mother, like puppy" holds true; therefore, it is important to meet the mother before adopting a puppy. A well-socialized mother, who is cared for properly by her breeder, has every chance of having well-adjusted puppies.

THE VET'S ADVICE

It is through contact with their mother that puppies learn to live in society with their fellow dogs, other animals, and humans. The recommended age for letting puppies go to their new homes is eight weeks, and you can even request that your puppy stay a few more weeks with his mother and siblings to further his initial training, especially if the environment in which they live is similar to your puppy's future environment.

Feeding

The brain's development and proper function requires a supply of various nutrients, such as docosahexaenoic acid (DHA: omega-3 fatty acid), an essential component of neuronal membranes. Increasing the mother's DHA intake during gestation and lactation improves her puppies' learning ability. In contrast, DHA deficiency affects the functioning of a puppy's brain, resulting in a decrease in learning ability (e.g., attention and memory disorders) and a disruption in exploratory behavior.

Rich in omega-3 fatty acids

THE VET'S ADVICE

During gestation, puppies ingest amniotic fluid in which certain food substances—in particular, aromatic substances such as herbs and flavorings—from their mother's diet are found. These same substances are also found in the mother's milk. Thus, depending on their mother's diet, puppies acquire certain food preferences.

a well-adjusted mother and, once adopted, by that of their owners, who will encourage them in their discovery of the world.

Training

The manner in which a puppy is trained will shape his perception of the world. Coercive training based on punishment will lead to distrust of humans, whereas positive training, which is based on encouragement and rewards, will establish a bond of trust between the puppy and his owner; it will facilitate the achievement of the puppy's full potential. This is the essence of positive training!

The Brain Is a Sponge

A puppy's brain is constantly active; it absorbs everything. Spontaneous activity formed by past experiences influences a puppy's behavior and perception of the world. If subjected to several negative emotions, a puppy will have difficulty feeling positive emotions, and vice versa. Thus, a puppy can become either a shy and timid adult or one who is happy and open to the world and to others. The earlier the negative emotions start, the greater the damage.

Social Relationships

At birth, a dog does not know that he is a dog. Identity construction, i.e., the way in which a dog defines and recognizes himself, develops in the initial weeks of his life, when he is in constant contact with his mother and littermates. If a young puppy is abandoned by his mother and is adopted by a cat, he will consider himself a cat; the same is applicable if he is adopted by humans. Therefore, some dogs prefer humans and refuse any contact with other dogs.

Leave me alone!

Hello!

Woof! Thanks, mom!

Experiences

From the third week of life, a puppy becomes sensitive to the stimuli of his environment and becomes curious; this is the socialization period. Each new experience generates fairly strong emotions. When the puppy feels overwhelmed, he seeks comfort from his mother. Thus, to successfully adapt to their future living environments, puppies must be immersed in a stimulating environment during their initial weeks, surrounded by the reassuring affection of

The Breed Does Not Make the Dog

A dog's personality is not determined by outward appearance, and love at first sight never lasts. More important than the breed is the close relationship that you will build with your dog and the positive training that you will give him, which will make him a well-adjusted, happy, obedient, and loving companion. However, a dog's skill set and physical makeup should correspond with his future tasks and environment. The following breed classifications are those of the Fédération Cynologique Internationale (FCI), the "world canine organization."

THE DIFFERENT BREEDS AND THEIR SKILLS

All dog breeds were initially selected by humans to assist them in different tasks: big game hunting, pest control, game spotting, guarding, pulling, herding, companionship, etc. Thus, they were classified into groups according to their skills and physical makeup. Although dogs no longer work as much today, they do retain certain abilities that they happily demonstrate if given the chance.

GROUP 1

SHEEPDOGS AND CATTLE DOGS (EXCEPT SWISS CATTLE DOGS)

Bouvier des Flanders

German Shepherd

GROUP 2

PINSCHERS AND SCHNAUZERS, MOLOSSOIDS, SWISS MOUNTAIN AND CATTLE DOGS

Rottweiler

Boxer

GROUP 3

TERRIERS

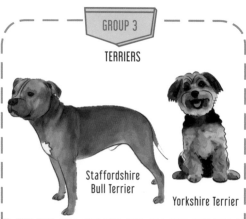

Staffordshire Bull Terrier

Yorkshire Terrier

GROUP 4

DACHSHUNDS

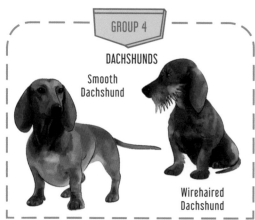

Smooth Dachshund

Wirehaired Dachshund

GROUP 5

SPITZ AND PRIMITIVE TYPES

Siberian Husky

German Spitz

GROUP 6

SCENTHOUNDS AND RELATED BREEDS

Basset Hound

Beagle

GROUP 7

POINTING DOGS

Weimaraner

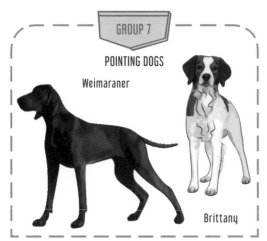

Brittany

GROUP 8

RETRIEVERS, FLUSHING DOGS, WATER DOGS

Golden Retriever

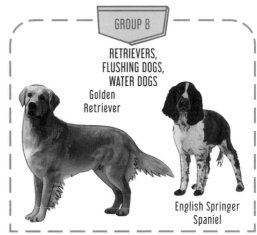

English Springer Spaniel

GROUP 9

COMPANION AND TOY DOGS

Cavalier King Charles Spaniel

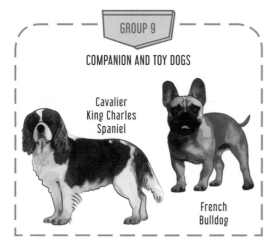

French Bulldog

GROUP 10

SIGHTHOUNDS

Italian Greyhound

Afghan Hound

SIMILAR YET SO DIFFERENT

A dog's behavior depends on both genes and environment. According to recent studies, of the 20,000 genes in the canine genome, approximately only 50 determine physical appearance (height at the withers, shape of the head, carriage of the ears and tail, length of the tail, color and texture of the coat, and so on). Therefore, two dogs of the same breed have only 0.25% of common genetic heritage. This tiny percentage of the dog's genetics does not make every dog of the same breed a carbon copy of the others. Between two lines of the same breed, there

It is impossible to predict behavior based on physical appearance alone.

angry

brave

sociable

timid

Judging me by my looks is like judging a book by its cover!

shy

playful

are sometimes more behavioral differences than between dogs of two different breeds altogether.

Dogs of the same breed are not clones, even though they may look very similar.

MAKE THE RIGHT CHOICE

If you want your dog to perform a specific task (tracking, hunting, herding, protection, etc.), choose the breed that best meets your criteria, and then visit the breeder to evaluate the parents' skills on the spot. This is by no means a 100% guarantee of your dog's future aptitude for work, but it can be a good indicator.

If the dog is intended for companionship, choose a breed whose primary purpose is companionship or a breed that is far removed from its primary skill, such as the Yorkshire Terrier. There is nothing worse for a working dog than being idle. If you want a companion dog of a working, herding, or sporting breed, choose a descendant from a line of conformation (show) champions rather than from a line of working champions. A Border Collie from a working line may want to gather his human "herd" like he would sheep; it's only natural!

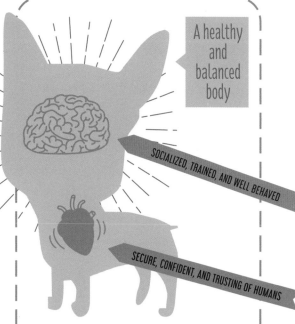

How About a Mixed Breed?

By choosing a mixed-breed puppy, particularly if you do not know his parents, you will not have any idea of his eventual physical characteristics or potential behavior as an adult. Regardless, you can make your dog the most wonderful companion by providing positive training. If you adopt a mixed-breed dog from a shelter, you will make him happy, and he will be grateful to you.

A healthy and balanced body

SOCIALIZED, TRAINED, AND WELL BEHAVED

SECURE, CONFIDENT, AND TRUSTING OF HUMANS

WHO IS MY DOG?

A dog is a body, a heart, and a mind. His training and learning are carried out according to these three components. Development must happen gradually and harmoniously. It must take place in such a way that the adult dog has a healthy body; is a well-adjusted, confident, and well-mannered member of society; and trusts humans. Therein lies the challenge of positive training!

Part 2

What Makes a Good Owner?

A good owner is a positive leader. To be a good owner, you must be your dog's best friend, work on self-improvement, remain realistic, identify and consider your dog's emotions, communicate with your dog, build a relationship of trust, establish clear and fair rules for your dog, and meet your dog's needs.

Be His Best Friend

Do not be an authoritarian and domineering master in competition with your dog but a loyal friend in whom he will have confidence and who he will follow with pleasure.

CHANGE YOUR PERCEPTION ABOUT DOGS

I'm your best friend. Follow me for the best life!

I am the leader. Do as I tell you and obey me; otherwise, watch out!

SIT!

OR

Good job!

LOVE YOUR DOG

Without love, you will not succeed in positive training. Love allows the puppy, deprived of his biological mother, to regain (with his new owner) that secure foundation that is essential to his cognitive development. Watching your dog, petting him, listening to him, communicating with him, helping him and encouraging his efforts, supporting him in his explorations, giving him your time, empathizing with him—all of this is part of positive training and essential to the realization of the dog's full potential.

ALL PUPPIES NEED IS LOVE

The dog who needs love the most is often the one who acts the least loving.

What dogs need most in their training costs us nothing but is often the most difficult for us to give them: time and attention.

BE AVAILABLE

Dogs do not raise themselves—or raise themselves badly—on their own. If you do not devote time, especially in the first few months, to your dog's training, socializaton, and recreational activities, you inevitably run the risk of his developing undesirable behavior.

TAKE HIS SKILLS INTO CONSIDERATION

According to their breed, dogs need to express certain instinctive behaviors (see Understand His Instincts, page 48). If your lifestyle does not allow you to provide your dog with these opportunities, you will have to redirect him to other, equally motivating activities. This is one of the keys to having a happy and well-adjusted dog. If you do not give your dog sufficient opportunities, he will figure out his own way to use his skills without worrying about whether it suits you.

For example, a Border Collie (a herding dog) is genetically programmed to round up and watch over livestock, and he has a strong motivation to do his job. In the absence of sheep or cows to be gathered, he will perform this bred-for task on humans unless you redirect his energy to an equally motivating activity, such as agility.

Did you see that pheasant?

Hurry and catch up with the herd!

Similarly, a bird dog will throw himself at a Frisbee or ball tossed by his owner—or, failing that, at the neighbor's chickens! And a pointing dog is never happier than when he does the job for which he was bred, even if the hunter comes home empty-handed!

I can't help it— I have to catch everything that flies!

Work on Improving Yourself

Before you demand perfection from your dog, start by asking yourself if you are a perfect owner. If not, take note of your mistakes and realize that they are opportunities for improvement—provided, of course, that you learn from them.

STAY IN CONTROL

A good teacher is a calm teacher. Your dog can detect anger in the way you communicate with him, and it may ruin your relationship with your dog.

For example, you want to teach your dog to come when called (see Coming When Called [Recall], page 120), but he has his nose stuck to the ground, concentrating on an interesting scent and ignoring you. **Do not get angry**. You are only discouraging your dog from coming to you when called, which can start a vicious cycle:

ANGER ➡ FEAR OF COMING TO YOU ➡ MORE ANGER ➡ MORE FEAR OF COMING TO YOU, AND SO ON

Instead, stay calm. Breathe, relax your muscles (you will not feel angry if your muscles stay relaxed), slowly count to at least ten to allow your dog to satisfy his need to sniff, and then resume your training, remembering to reward your dog every time he comes to you. If you cannot stay positive, end the training session.

Lie down!

What is she saying?

Don't expect too much too soon

EXPECTATION ⧺ POSSIBLE OUTCOME

BE REALISTIC

Do not expect perfection. All dogs are smart, but if you ask yours to learn to climb trees or stay in one place for an hour, you will certainly be disappointed!

Come here!

Before you can control your dog, you must control yourself.

Red face, rapid breathing, loud voice, teeth and hands clenched, perspiration, restlessness, muscle tension. You are angry!

Adapt your requests to suit his abilities.

To avoid frustrating your dog, do not ask him to do what he cannot reasonably do—for example, to be completely house-trained before six months of age or to understand a cue without showing him what it means. By asking your dog to do the impossible, you will prevent him from showing you what he can achieve.

Believe in your student and his abilities: the Pygmalion effect holds true for dogs, too!

Take his desires into account.

Know how to motivate your dog without using restraint or intimidation to get him to behave how you want. To do this, be assertive, choose win-win situations that benefit both you and your dog, and guide your dog toward the goal by considering his desires too so that he will obey of his own free will. Good owners are firm believers in the middle ground: they are neither passive nor aggressive, and they seek to establish relationships of trust with their dogs. This type of owner sees training as a game in which everyone wins.

GET HIS ATTENTION

Attention modulates brain activity and facilitates learning. The dog's attention span increases with age and training. A young puppy loves to switch activities.

To improve your puppy's concentration, train in a quiet place and gradually increase the duration (first two minutes, then five, then ten, then fifteen, and so on), which includes the time spent on distractions. It is better to have three five-minute lessons than just one fifteen-minute lesson. If your dog is tired or distracted, do not get angry but simply end the training session. The same applies to you. Always be focused on what you are doing.

WHAT YOU WANT — MIDDLE GROUND — WHAT YOUR DOG WANTS

- Help
- Understanding
- Trust
- Communication
- Guidance
- Harmony

sit! sit! sit!

The more disruptions from the outside world, the more distracted the dog will be, and the worse your training will go. Therefore, depending on the environment in which you're training, the dog may perceive the same cue in different ways.

What's all that noise?

When is playtime?

Great! There's my friend!

Demonstrate Empathy

Identifying, understanding, and considering the emotions felt by your dog are essential prerequisites for any training process. Indeed, the positive emotions generated by receiving rewards facilitate the dog's learning; negative emotions (such as fear or anger), on the other hand, can interfere with it.

IDENTIFY HIS EMOTIONS

A dog is a sensitive being, completely capable of feeling emotions. Your dog's emotions last for a short duration—from a few seconds to a few minutes (beyond that, they are referred to as "moods")—and are triggered by his perception of specific events and situations (e.g., fear of fireworks, pleasure in tasting a treat, joy in playing with children, sadness at the death of an animal companion). **Emotions lead to physiological** (e.g., urination, defecation, increased heart rate, dilated pupils) **and behavioral** (e.g., aggression, excitation, approach, escape, inhibition) reactions, combined with characteristic expressions, vocalizations, and postures.

Positive Emotions
Positive emotions indicate that the dog's safety, nutrition, and security needs are being met (see The Needs Pyramid, page 42). They convey a sense of well-being. Rewards generate positive emotions.

Negative Emotions
Negative emotions indicate that the dog's needs are not being met. They convey a sense of malaise. Punishment generates negative emotions.

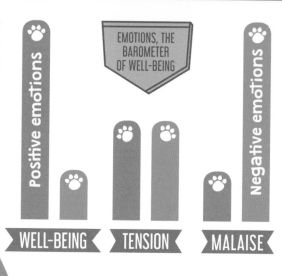

Positive emotions | Negative emotions

EMOTIONS, THE BAROMETER OF WELL-BEING

WELL-BEING | TENSION | MALAISE

ANGER
Frustration
Irritation
Exasperation
Fury

FEAR
Apprehension
Anxiety
Terror
Phobia

SADNESS
Defeat
Discouragement
Despair
Depression

JOY
Contentment
Satisfaction
Enthusiasm
Motivation

OBSERVE HIS FACIAL EXPRESSIONS AND POSTURES

Your dog's emotions are reflected in distinctive, easily identifiable facial expressions and postures.

JOY

1 The dog is sitting, with ears in a natural position, relaxed and slightly open mouth, tongue out, eyes wide open, and tail wagging.

2 The dog is in the "play bow," with ears in a natural position and gaze fixed on a toy or his owner. He barks as he wags his tail.

3 The dog is standing, alert, with ears in a natural position, mouth relaxed and slightly open, tongue out, eyes wide open, and tail wagging.

> Joy is a state of happiness, pleasure, and well-being resulting from the fulfillment of a need.

FEAR/ANXIETY

Low ears

Low posture, tail between legs

Trembling

Looking away

Crouching

Flattening

Licking lips with no food present

Keeping his distance

Running away

Refusing food

Fear is an emotion experienced in the face of a real and immediate danger or threat.

Keeping his distance

Anxiety is an emotion similar to fear but without a specific focus.

Slow gait

Yawning not caused by fatigue

Hypervigilance

Panting not related to thirst or heat

Sniffing ground when not actively hunting

Scratching for no reason

ANGER

Anger is a sudden reaction of dissatisfaction resulting from a threat or attack. It provokes the dog to act quickly, which can lead to aggression, especially if it is mixed with fear.

Fear and anger are often mixed.

2 **Low posture with ears drooping down,** lips curled, growling, and tail between legs.

1 **High posture with out-stretched limbs;** ears, hair along back, and tail upright; fixed gaze; and lips curled.

3 **Medium-low posture, with ears drooping down,** lips curled, growling or barking, and tail between legs.

> Sadness is a state of inaction or inhibition in the presence of inevitable harm or in the absence of something good.

SADNESS

The dog lacks spirit, sleeps a lot, eats less, lies around for hours doing nothing, keeps his eyes half-closed, and has a blank expression.

UNDERSTAND YOUR DOG'S EMOTIONS

Emotions are essential for survival.

What would happen to a dog who was not afraid of a predator? Fear causes increased blood flow to muscles in preparation for the flight response. However, emotions, especially negative emotions, can be harmful and detrimental to the dog's behavior when they are too frequent, intense, or unsuitable for the situation. A dog who fears children or his owner following abusive treatment is more likely to become aggressive. It is during the first months of his life that a puppy, confronted with different situations, learns to control his emotions, especially fear.

Emotions have particular functions.

Emotions dictate the dog's behavior. They are useful for the animal's survival and his quest for well-being.

Emotions	Needs
JOY	→ REWARD, MOTIVATE, CONNECT WITH OTHERS
FEAR	→ PREPARE TO FACE DANGER
ANGER	→ INTIMIDATE AN OPPONENT
SADNESS	→ ENCOURAGE COMPASSION AND SUPPORT, AVOID PAIN

The owner promotes his or her dog's positive emotions (e.g., joy) by meeting his needs and providing positive training.

Emotions communicate special needs.

There is always a hidden message in a dog's behavior.

Emotions	Needs
JOY	→ INTERACTION
FEAR	→ SECURITY
ANGER	→ CHANGE
SADNESS	→ COMFORT

A good owner identifies his or her dog's emotions to understand and respond to the dog's needs.

OBSERVING THE SITUATION

INTERPRETATION OF INFORMATION

NEED

EMOTIONS

BEHAVIOR

Know How to Communicate

Communication is the process, implemented voluntarily or involuntarily, by which we transmit messages to others. You cannot avoid communicating with your dog. Whether you like it or not, your dog "scrutinizes" you with his eyes, ears, and nose wide open, even when you are not talking to him. A word, silence, a blink, a hand movement, a sigh of relief, your scent—everything sends a message, and nothing escapes our dogs.

THE CHANNELS OF COMMUNICATION

The conscious or unconscious messages you send to your dog pass through different channels: verbal (words), paraverbal (intonation, rhythm, inflection, voice intensity), and nonverbal (gestures, postures, expressions). Each channel provides information, and the sum of this information makes up the message. Paraverbal and nonverbal channels, when well mastered, reinforce verbal messages. Although you may not always be conscious of it, these channels also provide information about your mood by indicating whether you are happy, annoyed, angry, etc., in addition to how/what you are feeling toward your dog: affectionate, indifferent, trusting, suspicious, and so on.

Paraverbal and nonverbal channels are essential to effective communication.

The difficulty of communication lies in the fact that most of a message is conveyed through nonverbal communication, which, unlike verbal communication, is difficult to master. If you are angry with your dog, do not hide it; the dog knows it! You should be calm and relaxed when you try to teach recall.

	IMPORTANCE	MASTERY	RELIABILITY	
VERBAL	Weak	Strong	Weak	MESSAGE
PARAVERBAL	Average	Average	Average	
NONVERBAL	Strong	Weak	Strong	

Communication
is 5% what you say
and 95% how you say it.

VERBAL — Words

PARA-VERBAL — Intonation, rhythm, inflection, intensity of voice

NONVERBAL — Gestures, postures, gaze, facial expressions, head movements, gait, speed of movement, distance, physical contact

MESSAGE

In instances where conflicting messages are conveyed by several communication channels, the dog prioritizes the messages transmitted by the paraverbal and nonverbal channels.

INCONSISTENT MESSAGES

VERBAL: "I am your friend" ➡ friendly

PARAVERBAL: loud voice ➡ aggressive

NONVERBAL: increasing speed of movement ➡ aggressive

CONSISTENT MESSAGES

VERBAL: "I am your friend" ➡ friendly

PARAVERBAL: soft tone of voice ➡ friendly

NONVERBAL: slow movement ➡ friendly

INCONSISTENT MESSAGES

VERBAL: "You are the most handsome dog" ➡ affectionate

PARAVERBAL: loud voice ➡ aggressive

NONVERBAL: no respect for personal space ➡ aggressive

CONSISTENT MESSAGES

VERBAL: "You are the most handsome dog" ➡ affectionate

PARAVERBAL: whispering ➡ affectionate

NONVERBAL: gentle touch ➡ affectionate

Give Clear Cues

Giving your dog a cue is a complex process that involves five steps, the knowledge and mastery of which make it possible to obtain the desired behavior or, if not, to make the necessary adjustments.

1. ENCODING

This consists of associating the cue with a coded message that the dog can understand by using the three communication channels (verbal, paraverbal, and nonverbal).

Verbal Channel
The verbal message consists of one or more key words. Make the verbal cue short and clear and link it to a specific behavior: "come," "heel," "sit," "down," "play dead," and the like.

The Paraverbal Channel
Paraverbal messages are conveyed by the flow, tone, and intensity of your voice. You must clearly articulate each word while speaking neither too fast nor too slow.

• **To give a cue,** use a medium tone of voice and low intensity, making adjustments to suit the distance between you and your dog and accounting for any distractions. Be relaxed and be confident in your dog's ability to succeed. Never forget that your voice conveys your mood and your feelings toward your pet.

• **To show joy** and reward your dog, use a higher tone of voice with more intensity.

• **To demonstrate your assertiveness** and your self-confidence, use a low tone of voice with low intensity. Never yell at your dog. Getting angry and frightening him just weakens your relationship.

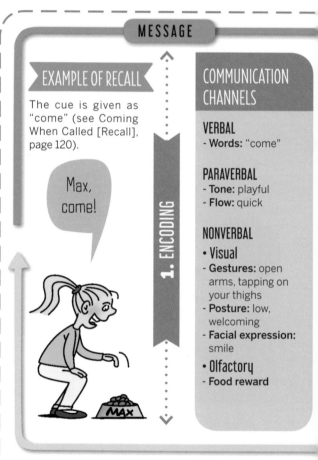

MESSAGE

EXAMPLE OF RECALL

The cue is given as "come" (see Coming When Called [Recall], page 120).

Max, come!

1. ENCODING

COMMUNICATION CHANNELS

VERBAL
- **Words:** "come"

PARAVERBAL
- **Tone:** playful
- **Flow:** quick

NONVERBAL
• **Visual**
- **Gestures:** open arms, tapping on your thighs
- **Posture:** low, welcoming
- **Facial expression:** smile
• **Olfactory**
- **Food reward**

Nonverbal Channel

Nonverbal messages are conveyed through gestures, postures, gaze, and facial expressions.

2. TRANSMISSION

Once transmitted, the coded message may be altered by auditory, visual, or olfactory interference from the environment. A quiet environment with few distractions will facilitate better communication.

3. PERCEPTION

Once the message reaches the dog, it is perceived through the dog's various sensory organs. Poor vision, poor hearing, or an impaired sense of smell can disrupt the dog's reception of the message.

4. DECODING

Once perceived, the message is decoded by passing through the dog's mental filters (i.e., mood, personality, experiences, motivation, relationship with you). The better the relationship of trust between you and your dog, the easier, more instantaneous, and more precise the communication will be (see Build a Relationship of Trust, page 38).

5. ACTION AND FEEDBACK

Communication is circular. Giving a cue involves a sender (you), a receiver (the dog), and a message that, once decoded, leads to an action (feedback), allowing you to gauge whether your message has been understood and then to act accordingly.

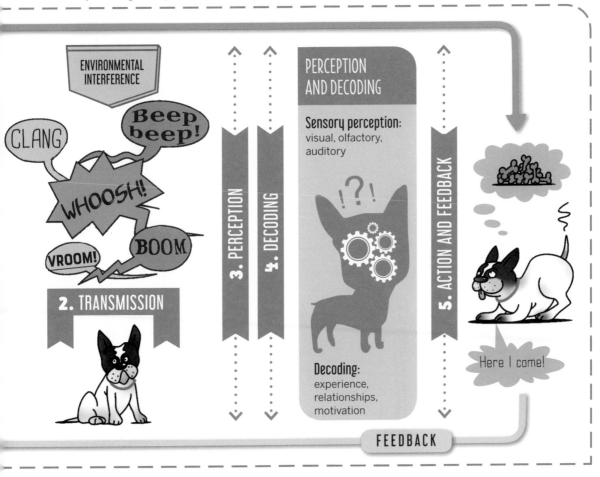

If your dog comes to you (positive feedback), he will receive the promised reward.

If your dog does not obey (negative feedback), you will have to consider the following:
• clarity of your message (encoding)
• various distractions that may have interfered with the message's transmission
• your dog's sensory skills that may have affected his perception of the message
• his mental filters used in decoding the message
If you can determine why your dog misunderstood the message, you can make the necessary adjustments next time you give the cue.

NONVERBAL COMMUNICATION

Gestures

For each cue, use a gesture specific to that cue. Choose simple gestures that combine arm and hand movements. Once you have associated an action with a cue, do not change it.

Thanks to a dog's excellent ability to distinguish between various movements, you can communicate with your dog from a distance with simple hand signals.

STAY!

STOP!

SIT!

DOWN!

Posture

To show your assertiveness and self-confidence, stand up straight, with your feet flat on the ground, head and shoulders square and facing forward. Breathe calmly. To look less imposing and more welcoming, squat down.

SHOW YOUR SELF-CONFIDENCE

ASSUME A WELCOMING POSTURE

Gaze

Have a confident and caring look. Look at your dog without staring into his eyes (he may feel uncomfortable); instead, steady your gaze on his forehead or back. You can also use your gaze to give your dog information, for example, by looking at him first and then at the object you want him to fetch.

Facial Expressions

Initially neutral, your face should light up with a wide smile when your dog behaves as desired.

> The owner who does not master communication lives with his or her dog as if they were strangers.

IMPROVE THE WAY YOU COMMUNICATE YOUR CUES

On the basis of the dog's action (feedback), you can then determine whether you communicated your given cue successfully and make any necessary adjustments. Let us use the example of recall (Come cue).

1. Positive feedback: the dog comes cheerfully to you, wagging his tail (positive emotion).

When the communication is perfect, the dog understands your message and thus comes to you with pleasure. He certainly deserves his food reward and petting.

2. Negative feedback: the dog stays put, continues what he was doing, or runs away.

Communication is poor. There are several possible reasons for this.

• **The message is incomprehensible.** You did not link the command to a specific behavior. It is pointless to shout "come" to your dog if you have not already associated the act of coming to you with the verbal cue "come" (see Coming When Called [Recall], page 120). Review encoding (the first step of communication).

• **The message is inconsistent.** You ask your dog to come to you, but your focus is on a text message from your boss, and you are not paying attention to what is happening at present. Or maybe you are acting annoyed or angry, and your mood is telling the dog to stay away. Your dog is not stupid! Review encoding (the first step of communication).

• **Distractions are interfering with the message.** Noise from passersby or cars or the presence of hedges/trees can interfere with your dog's auditory and visual perception of the message. Review the second step of communication (transmission) by changing the environment.

• **The dog still does not receive the message.** Work on the third step (perception). Or, your dog might have a hearing problem. If so, you will need to improve your nonverbal encoding.

• **The dog lacks motivation.** He saw a rabbit in the bushes and would rather chase it than come to you. Or maybe your male dog sniffed out a female dog in heat and chooses her instead of you, which is quite natural (see The Needs Pyramid, page 42). Work on the second step (transmission) by changing the environment or on the fourth step (decoding) by increasing motivation with the promise of a great reward.

• **The dog remembers unpleasant experiences.** The last time he came to you, you immediately put him on leash to go home, or, worse, you punished him for not responding right away. Work on the fourth step, and change the training method. Communication will not be effective without a relationship of trust.

Positive or negative feedback

The manner in which the command is transmitted affects how your dog feels.

Heel!

Positive feedback

Negative feedback

Negative feedback

Build a Relationship of Trust

A relationship of trust is the foundation of positive training. It must be established as early as possible, constantly enriched, and renewed throughout the dog's life. The use of intimidation or coercion teaches the dog to fear his owner. It generates negative emotions, such as fear, and undermines the relationship of trust. It leads the dog to perceive the world as hostile and threatening and to adopt behaviors aimed at reassuring himself and/or allowing him to avoid physical confrontation.

To build a relationship of trust with your dog, make sure that the sum of your interactions (positive, negative, or neutral) is leaning toward the positive side. To this end, you should share pleasant activities with your dog every day (walking, playing games, agility), show him your affection (sweet words, cuddles, pettiing), understand him, know how to communicate with him, choose a positive training method (based on cooperation, motivation, reward, and encouragement), and fulfill his needs. Otherwise, you risk developing a relationship based on mistrust, with the dog exhibiting behaviors of avoidance, fear, and sometimes aggression.

Sit! Sit! Sit!

I'm afraid...

Trembling
Dilated pupils
Low ears
Low tail
Panting

TILT THE BALANCE OF INTERACTIONS

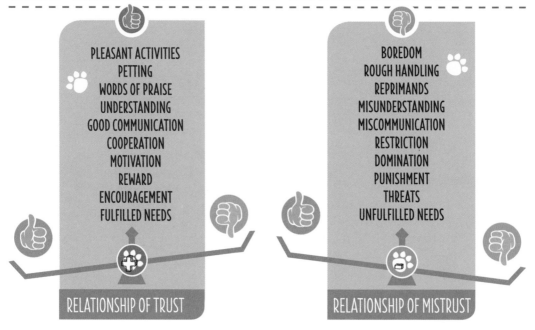

PLEASANT ACTIVITIES
PETTING
WORDS OF PRAISE
UNDERSTANDING
GOOD COMMUNICATION
COOPERATION
MOTIVATION
REWARD
ENCOURAGEMENT
FULFILLED NEEDS

RELATIONSHIP OF TRUST

BOREDOM
ROUGH HANDLING
REPRIMANDS
MISUNDERSTANDING
MISCOMMUNICATION
RESTRICTION
DOMINATION
PUNISHMENT
THREATS
UNFULFILLED NEEDS

RELATIONSHIP OF MISTRUST

INCREASE THE DOG'S TRUST RESERVOIR

The importance of your dog's trust in you can be compared to a water tank filled with buckets of positive interactions and drained of negative interactions.

POSITIVE INTERACTIONS

RESERVOIR OF TRUST

NEGATIVE INTERACTIONS

Your dog forgets nothing.

Dogs never forget the experiences they have with their owners, especially when they are associated with strong positive or negative emotions; they will live with these memories for the rest of their lives. Like a computer, the dog's brain records these events, but, unlike a computer, a dog's brain cannot be reformatted. Thus, over time, either a relationship of affinity and love or one of mistrust and insecurity will develop between the dog and his human. Your story with your dog is unique; do not spoil it by failing to show love toward your dog.

THE VET'S ADVICE

Without training and positive interactions with you, and when you leave your dog alone for long hours at home, it precludes you from establishing a relationship of trust. Neglect is a form of abuse and is detrimental to the dog's behavioral development. Frustrated by the inability to build a relationship with his human, the dog can experience conflict with those around him and adopt disruptive behavior, such as barking, destructiveness, running away, and unclean bathroom habits. Establishing a close relationship with your dog takes time. Before adopting a dog, ask yourself if you will have enough time to devote to him.

Establish Clear and Fair Rules

To properly train your dog, you must, from the outset, establish clear and fair rules that are accepted and followed by the entire family. These rules are essential to the dog's safety and development. They specify the behavior expected of the dog in given situations. Rules are essential for the dog's stability and to allow you and your dog to coexist harmoniously.

RULE 1:

He must ask politely. Whatever the dog wants from you (food, to go outside to play, his toy), he must first show good manners by sitting calmly. It is a rule of courtesy, so to speak. At first, you will give him the Sit cue and reward him until sitting becomes an automatic behavior.

RULE 2:

What is allowed today will be allowed tomorrow; what is forbidden today will be forbidden tomorrow. Enforce the rules consistently, every day, for each desirable or undesirable behavior. Do not reward your dog by petting him when he jumps on you while you are sitting in your chair only to reprimand him the next time he jumps up when his paws are muddy or your arms are full. Do not feed your dog at the table only to push him away when your boss comes over for dinner.

This doesn't make sense!

Hello, I'm here!

Good boy! I like polite manners.

The best way to get something is to sit in front my owner.

RULE 3:

All good behavior deserves a reward, even if it is spontaneous, whereas undesirable behavior should never be rewarded (see Extinction, page 188), whatever the situation. Instead, interrupt your dog and redirect him toward the desired behavior (see Positive Modification, page 187).

RULE 4:

Every well-trained dog must earn his "treat." Give your dog part of his food ration in exchange for nothing (freely) and the other part as a reward for his good

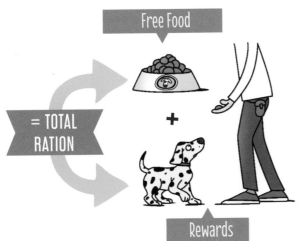

Free Food + Rewards = TOTAL RATION

Involve the whole family. In a family, all members influence each other. The dog reacts to the behaviors of others but others also influence the dog's behavior. To have a well-adjusted and well-behaved dog, it is not enough to be a positive leader; it is also necessary for good communication to exist within the family and that your concept of training is shared by all family members. For example, if the established rule is not to feed the dog at the table, all family members must respect it.

Therefore, before adopting a dog, it is important to ensure that everyone shares the same training expectations and approach. Moreover, sometimes your dog's behavior reveals inconsistency among family members that must be resolved.

behavior, so that, by the end of the day, your dog gets his full food ration. Spontaneous good behavior is rewarded in the same way as the good behavior you request during training. This way of distributing food puts you in a positive leadership position.

A positive leader is an owner who the dog obeys not through coercion or intimidation but by choice, because he knows that his owner only wants good things for him. There is no competition between dog and owner but, instead, healthy and fruitful cooperation.

> In a family, the behavior of each person influences the behavior of the others.

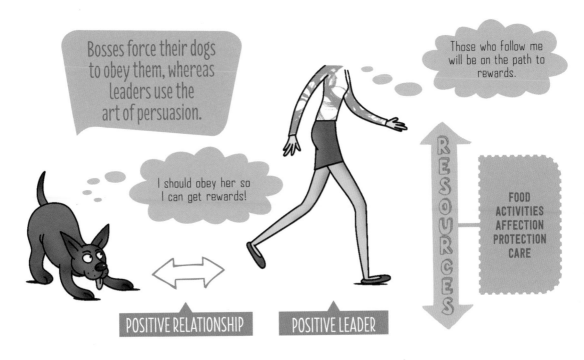

Bosses force their dogs to obey them, whereas leaders use the art of persuasion.

Those who follow me will be on the path to rewards.

I should obey her so I can get rewards!

RESOURCES

FOOD
ACTIVITIES
AFFECTION
PROTECTION
CARE

POSITIVE RELATIONSHIP

POSITIVE LEADER

Meet His Basic Needs

A good owner is attentive to the well-being and happiness of his or her dog. The owner knows what the dog needs and ensures that these needs are met, giving priority to basic needs, such as water and food.

THE VET'S ADVICE

If your dog drinks and urinates a lot, consult your veterinarian to have his blood glucose and kidney function assessed by a blood test.

HYDRATION

Water is essential for life. A dog's body is made up of about 80% water. The dog must drink water regularly to compensate for losing water due to panting, perspiration, relieving himself, and the like. A dog gets some of his water from his food. If your dog eats dry food (kibble), he should consume about 2 ounces (60 ml) of water per pound (0.45 kg) of body weight per day. This quantity varies according to the dog's activity level and the climate. This requirement is higher for

THE NEEDS PYRAMID

A dog's needs can be classified according to their importance. The most important ones are at the bottom of the pyramid. These are the biggest priority for you to meet.

THE NEED TO BE USEFUL AND LEARN

SOCIAL AND RECREATIONAL NEEDS: socialization with humans and other dogs, affection, play, canine sports (e.g., agility)

INSTINCTIVE NEEDS: reproduction, hunting, chewing

SAFETY NEEDS: to feel protected, to be understood, trust in his owner

BASIC NEEDS: drinking, eating, eliminating, health care, sleep

A DOG'S BODY IS COMPOSED OF 80% WATER.

100
75
50
25
0

H_2O

❓ IS YOUR DOG DEHYDRATED?

SYMPTOMS OF DEHYDRATION
• Sunken eyes
• Lethargy
• Loss of appetite
• Dry mouth and eyes
• Positive skin fold test

HOW TO DO THE SKIN FOLD TEST
• Pinch the skin on the back of the neck, between the shoulders.
• Gently lift it to a height of about 2 inches (5 cm).
• Release the skin.
• Hydrated skin instantly returns to its original position; if it does not, the dog is dehydrated.

How should daily rations be distributed?

To keep the dog busy looking for food and to stimulate his intelligence, place 25% of his daily ration in a food-dispensing toy, a slow-feeder bowl, or his environment (the yard or a cardboard box).

To motivate the dog during training, reserve 25% of his daiy ration to use as training rewards. Many owners use a "treat bag" to have food rewards handy during training sessions. Earning food is totally normal for a dog!

Give the dog the rest of his food (50%) at regularly scheduled mealtimes: four times a day up to four months old, then three times a day up to six months old, and then twice a day.

puppies and lactating females. If your dog eats wet food, he will not need to drink as much water, as these foods contain water.

Make sure that your dog has fresh water available at all times and check the amount of water he drinks.

Food-dispensing toys: the dog would rather search for his food than have it available. These toys force your dog to use his brain to get his food and keep him busy in your absence.

FEEDING

The puppy's first teeth appear at three weeks of age, at which point he begins to take an interest in food other than breast milk. The breeder will give him a weaning mush made of puppy kibble and water, gradually reducing the amount of water mixed with the kibble.

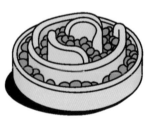

Slow-feeder bowls: these bowls make it more challenging to pick up the kibble, which slows down food intake and improves digestion.

Weaning is complete when the puppy can do without breast milk, around the seventh or eighth week. When the puppy is weaned, he needs a daily ration of dog food, calculated according to breed, size, and age. Until adulthood (when his weight is stable), weigh your puppy weekly and ensure that he is gaining weight and growing well.

🐾➕ THE VET'S ADVICE

A breeder should keep puppies for at least eight weeks before letting them go to new homes. If you buy a puppy from a breeder, he will already be weaned and will be eating a nutritious puppy food. Because good nutrition is the best preventive medicine, choose a premium diet that suits your dog's age and size and is recommended by your veterinarian.

Choose the right food bowl.

• For a large dog: elevated to improve comfort.
• For a dog with long ears: deep, narrow, with elevated edges to prevent the dog's ears from getting soaked in the bowl.
• For a dog with a flat/short nose: shallow, with low edges and a grooved bottom; makes it easier to pick up food and avoids putting pressure on the throat.
• For a dog with a long nose: deep, wide, with elevated edges; creates space for the nose.
• For a puppy: shallow, with low edges; makes it easier to reach the food and avoids putting pressure on the throat.

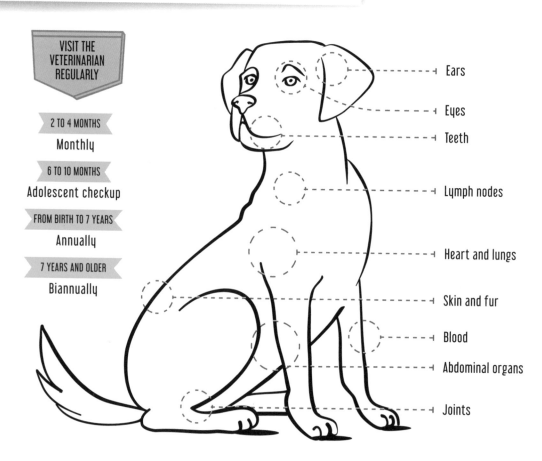

VISIT THE VETERINARIAN REGULARLY

2 TO 4 MONTHS
Monthly

6 TO 10 MONTHS
Adolescent checkup

FROM BIRTH TO 7 YEARS
Annually

7 YEARS AND OLDER
Biannually

- Ears
- Eyes
- Teeth
- Lymph nodes
- Heart and lungs
- Skin and fur
- Blood
- Abdominal organs
- Joints

HOUSE-TRAINING

Take your puppy out to potty at regular times; the younger the puppy, the more frequently he will need to go out (see House-Training, page 118). The more often you take your dog out, the more comfortable he will be, and the sooner he will be clean indoors.

BE HEALTHY

Have a regular care routine at home.
• Brush your dog's teeth every day.
• Give him quality food.
• Give him vet-recommended preventives to protect him from external and intestinal parasites.

Protect him with vaccinations.
Vaccinations are an essential form of protection. The protocol can vary according to the dog's risk of certain diseases, lifestyle, and health status. The first vaccines are given at approximately six to eight weeks, with booster shots given at three- to four-week intervals. Once the initial vaccination series is complete, the dog typically gets annual booster shots.

There are vaccines against many diseases, including canine distemper, parvovirus, infectious canine hepatitis, kennel cough, leptospirosis, rabies, and Lyme disease.

Should problems arise, be sure to consult the vet immediately.

If your dog has any of the following symptoms, consult your veterinarian right away:
– Difficulty breathing
– Vision problems
– Bleeding
– Poisoning
– Abnormal urination
– Whimpering
– Stomach pain
– Loss of appetite
– Vomiting or diarrhea
– Behavioral changes

THE VET'S ADVICE

A lack of or excess of sleep can be indicative of a behavioral developmental disorder.

SLEEP

Sleep, during the initial months of life, permits brain development and maturation (by establishing neural connections) as well as the solidification of what the puppy has learned because, during sleep, the brain replays the day's activities. Sleep duration decreases with age. An adult dog sleeps between eight and ten hours a day (or even much more if he lacks activity and is bored). For your dog's comfort, provide him with a soft bed where he can lie down and stretch out. Above all, do not wake your dog up when he is asleep!

For the first few nights, if your puppy cannot stand being alone, which is often the case, bring his bed or crate into your room. After a few weeks, when he has become accustomed to spending time in his crate during the day, you can let him sleep there alone at night. If, despite all your efforts, your dog still has trouble sleeping alone, stay in the room with him and then go back to your room once he is asleep.

Provide for His Safety

Your dog needs a safe space of his own; this means a doghouse, bed, or area where no one will disturb or punish him and a secure environment where he won't get hurt—especially for a puppy, who has the annoying tendency of exploring everything with his mouth. You need to take basic safety precautions in each room in the house as well as the garage and the yard.

IN THE KITCHEN

- When cooking, always use the rear burners in case your dog jumps up and puts his paws on the stove.
- Keep items that could be chewed and/or swallowed out of reach (strings, twist ties, elastic bands, plastic bags).
- Do not leave knives on the table.
- If your dog knows how to open cabinet doors, use child safety locks to secure them.
- When using cleaning chemicals, keep your dog out of the room to prevent him from inhaling toxic fumes.
- Install a safety gate to keep your dog out of the kitchen when you do not want to be disturbed.

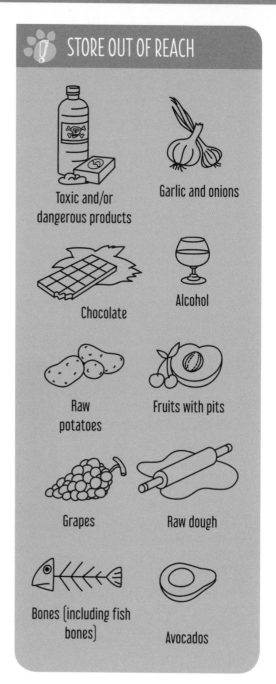

STORE OUT OF REACH

Toxic and/or dangerous products

Garlic and onions

Chocolate

Alcohol

Raw potatoes

Fruits with pits

Grapes

Raw dough

Bones (including fish bones)

Avocados

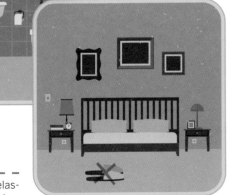

IN THE BEDROOM

• Place your jewelry, hearing aids, and other small objects in a closed box, out of reach.
• Do not leave socks, shoes, or laundry lying around, as they may look like chew toys.

IN THE YARD AND OUTDOORS

• Install a fence around your yard to prevent your dog from running away or being attacked by other dogs.
• In extremely hot weather, avoid walking your dog on the hot sidewalk.
• Always provide your dog with a bowl of fresh, clean water outdoors.
• Your dog should have a shaded area to protect him from the sun and a doghouse to protect him from the rain and cold.

IN THE BATHROOM

• Store cleaning products, elastic hair ties, and dental floss in a cupboard out of reach.
• Empty the bathtub when you leave the room to avoid any risk of drowning.
• If your dog knows how to open cabinet doors, use child safety locks.
• Close the toilet lid so that your dog does not drink the water, especially if you use chemical cleaning products.
• Store medications in a securely closed medicine cabinet, out of reach.

IN THE LIVING ROOM

• In a closed drawer, store pins, tacks, paper clips, USBs, rubber bands, etc.
• Keep matches out of reach; protect the fireplace with a fireplace screen.
• Do not leave cigarettes or electronic cigarette refills lying around.
• Unplug electrical cords when not in use and put them out of reach so that they cannot be chewed.

IN THE GARAGE

• To avoid poisoning, keep batteries, rock salt, antifreeze (which is very appealing to dogs), and garden pesticides out of reach.
• Discard old Styrofoam packaging material, which can cause digestive blockages if ingested.

Some behaviors, such as chewing on computer wires, chasing the neighbor's chickens, or digging under the fence to meet up with a female dog in heat, are considered bad behaviors to be suppressed, but they are only based on natural canine instincts.

HUNTING

Although dogs no longer need to hunt to ensure their daily bread, they retain within them this instinct of observation, pursuit, and capture. If your dog does not have the opportunity to hunt birds or mammals (squirrels, rabbits, wild boar, deer, etc.) in the wild, you can offer him prey substitutes, such as balls, toys, or Frisbees that you throw for him to catch and then bring back to you. The advantage of this activity is that your dog will probably get tired long before you do!

CHEWING

Chewing is an activity that calms the dog, occupies his mind, strengthens his jaws, and maintains his teeth. A dog's diet in the wild once required him to chew for long hours, but this is no longer the case with manufactured dog food that can be swallowed greedily. If your dog does not have a proper object to chew on, he may use something in his environment (old shoe, child's toy, stuffed animal, chair leg, piece of wood). Therefore, it is essential to always make a variety of sturdy chew toys available to your dog. Choose toys that are specially designed for this purpose, appropriate to his size and strength. Avoid chews that are not easily digestible and are potentially dangerous, such as rawhides and raw bones.

BREEDING

Unless you are a breeder, it's very likely that you will not want your dog to breed. The strong motivation associated with this act makes it difficult to suppress. A male dog in the prime of life, who smells the pheromones emitted by a female dog in heat, will have an irrepressible desire to run away and find her. Unless you want to deal with the consequences of raising puppies and placing them in good homes, you should consider having your male neutered or your female spayed.

Provide Socialization and Recreation

A dog is happy when he shares activities with his humans or other members of his species. These connections are essential to the dog's happiness and development. If you have to leave your dog alone for a long time, hire a dog sitter.

AFFECTION

You love your dog—nothing can be more normal! So show him love. Physical contact is the best way to show your affection, strengthen your friendship, enrich the relationship, calm the dog, give him confidence, check for good condition, and, above all, treat him well because this stimulates the production of endorphins (pleasure hormones) and oxytocin (love hormone). Most dogs love to be petted.

Not all physical contact is equal. Instead of petting your dog in a hurry, give him a real massage from time to time (see page 50).

TIME WITH FRIENDS

A dog is not meant to remain alone with his owner. During the socialization period (see Socialization, page 103), dogs learn to "speak dog" as well as make friends with other species. For these intra- and interspecies friendships to continue, make sure that your dog participates in regular activities in the park, in the neighborhood, in the agility club, and the like, with all of his friends (dogs, humans, and—why not?—other types of animals).

Playing with other dogs maintains canine friendships. Dogs delight in meeting their dog friends in the park. This provides an opportunity to perfect their "dogspeak." Plus, meeting people other than their owners is also always a joy for well-socialized dogs.

Learn Canine Massage

Gentle massage, begun at an early age, teaches the puppy to like physical contact and paves the way for subsequent handling for grooming and medical care. It stimulates the cutaneous nerves, provides relaxation and well-being, and makes it possible for the owner to detect certain anomalies (presence of parasites, pain, abnormal masses).

HOW TO START

• Gradually increase the duration of the massages.
• Massage the dog alone, in a quiet place.
• Massage with warm hands.
• Gradually increase the pressure.
• If your dog does not like it, reduce the pressure or stop the session.
• Perform only superficial massages; deep massages are not always pleasant, have therapeutic indications, and must be performed by a professional, such as the veterinarian.

Here are some examples that are easy to do at home (inspired by the gentle massage techniques developed by Linda Tellington-Jones).

EAR MASSAGE

Gently massage the ears from the base to the tip, placing your fingers on different areas of the outer ear.

HEAD MASSAGE

Massage the skin of the head with circular movements.

Provides pleasure

Enriches the relationship

Keeps the dog in shape

Gets the dog used to physical contact

MASSAGE

Allows the owner to detect abnormalities

Reduces stress and nervousness

LIMB MASSAGE

 **1** Hold the limb with your hand. Slightly rub the skin upward. Pause for several seconds.

 **2** Gently lower your hand and let the skin return to its regular position.

 **3** Place your hand a little lower and start again.

BACK MASSAGE

 1 **Massage in a circular motion.** Hold your hand in a loose fist and massage with your knuckles.

Continue down the length of the back, making small circles. Your fingers and the dog's skin must move together.

2 **Massage in a zigzag.** Place your closed hand at the dog's neckline. Go down along the back by tracing a zigzag, alternately opening and closing your hand.

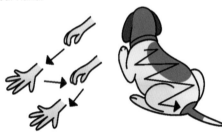

> Be creative! You can invent your own massages, as long as your dog enjoys them.

BODY MASSAGE

1 **Massage in a circular motion.** Place your fingertips on your dog's skin. Keep your thumb in place and make small circles with the other fingers. Do not slide your fingers on the coat; you must move the skin.

2 **Massage smoothly.** Place your hand flat on the shoulder. Glide your hand in the direction of the fur, along the body, to the ends of the legs and tail.

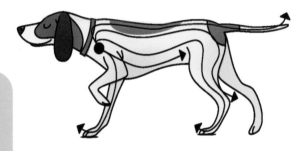

Provide Physical Activity

In the absence of a real job, physical exercise is essential to both the dog's balance and yours. This should motivate you! Underestimating a dog's need for physical exercise is one of the main causes of undesirable behavior.

BASIC ACTIVITIES

Walking

Walking is an ideal activity for many companion dogs but not rigorous enough for high-energy dogs. Try to go for at least three half-hour-long walks every day. For the dog's enjoyment, vary the scenery (city, countryside, woods, beach, mountains) when you can and, from time to time, allow him to sniff and explore as he wishes.

Playing in the Park

Off-leash dog parks provide fun social interaction for well-behaved dogs. If your dog has a dog friend, arrange a playdate so they can have fun together; dogs love to run and chase! You can also bring toys (see Hunting, p. 48) for them to play with. Spending an hour at the park every day is a real treat for many dogs.

Swimming

Your dog's swimming ability will depend on his breed and body type. Swimming is a sport that will not harm a dog's joints (very useful for rehabilitation) and is more intense exercise than walking. Dog pools are available (check with your veterinarian for information). Your dog can also swim in your own pool or in a safe body of water. For a beginner, equip him with a life jacket for his safety.

GAMES OF ALL KINDS

For dogs, play is the best reward. It is also a way of strengthening your relationship, teaching him self-control, and satisfying his craving for activity. All games, whatever they are, start and end when you decide, with the dog behaving calmly (dog in sitting position).

• Play cat-and-mouse with your dog.

• Play fetch with a ball or any other object, or play tug with a rope.

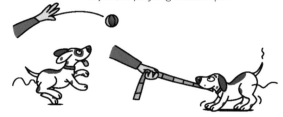

• A dog can also play on his own, for example, with treat-dispensing toys. You can also stimulate the dog's sense of smell by hiding treats in his surroundings.

Click!

• Just like playing games, learning in a fun and cheerful atmosphere with a lot of rewards is a delightful experience.

COMPETITIVE SPORTS

Agility

Inspired by equestrian jumping, this sport from England consists of guiding your dog through an obstacle course with your cues, without a leash or collar. The obstacles include hurdles, tire jumps, a dog walk, an A-frame, flexible or rigid tunnels, weave poles, and more. It requires both good physical condition and knowledge of many basic exercises.

Canicross

This sport consists of running cross-country equipped with a waist belt or a harness that is connected by an elastic, shock-absorbing tether, which reduces the impact on both the human body and the dog's harness when he pulls. There are two other versions of this sport: cani-walks (for walking) and bikejoring (for biking).

Disc Dog

This sport consists of throwing a Frisbee to the dog, who pursues it and catches it, often by performing spectacular tricks high in the air. Popular in the United States, this discipline is catching on in other countries.

Canine Freestyle

Popular in the United Kingdom under the name "heelwork to music," this sport was launched in the 1980s in Great Britain by Mary Ray. Dogs are required to follow their owners' dance routines and perform obedience exercises to music.

Allow Him to Learn and Be Useful

Loving your dog means discovering all of his talents.

cues, teach your dog to do fun tricks, such as play dead, sit pretty, and give high fives (see pages 151-159), and offer him educational toys at any age.

BEING USEFUL

Some breeds have been bred for particular skills (guarding and protecting, retrieving game, tracking game, flushing game, gathering herds, and so on). Once trained, dogs are happy when they can practice the work for which they have been bred. You can also teach them to perform other jobs, such as putting away their toys or fetching slippers or the newspaper. All they want to do is help.

Learning strengthens the relationship between dog and owner and allows the dog to gain self-confidence.

LEARNING

A dog's learning potential is immense. For instance, Chaser, a female Border Collie, succeeded in memorizing the names of more than 1,000 toys, which she could bring on cue. Without going that far, you can, apart from the basic

YOUR DOG'S SCHEDULE

Provide a schedule for your dog not only to keep him occupied but also to enable him to fulfill various needs. Some activities are vital (eating, drinking) and are a priority; others are secondary (learning, doing a job) yet essential. A puppy's schedule revolves mainly around house-training, while an adult dog's schedule depends on age, temperament, activity level, and breed. For example, a small pet dog, such as a Chihuahua, or a senior dog will obviously not have the same needs as a working dog (such as a Border Collie) in the prime of life.

    Before choosing a breed, research carefully. When choosing a puppy, get advice from the breeders and observe the puppy's parents. If you plan to leave your

> Providing your dog with a schedule that allows him to satisfy all of his needs is essential, especially since his living conditions are artificially constrained.

dog crated for eight hours a day, either do not bother adopting a dog or do not be surprised if he exhibits destructive behavior. Dogs need to get rid of their excess energy.

WHAT MAKES A GOOD OWNER?

Identify
and understand your
dog's emotions

Love your dog

Build a relationship
of trust

Fulfill
your dog's needs

Good owner
=
positive leader

Give
clear cues

Establish clear and
fair rules

Be available

Be
realistic

Know how to
communicate

Exercise
self-control

Is Your Dog Happy?

Because of domestication, dogs have become dependent on humans. Thus, our first duty is to make them happy. Even if this duty is not yet law, perhaps one day it will be. It would only be fair to show our gratitude for all of the benefits that dogs' companionship has brought us over the millennia.

A happy dog has a caring owner who takes care of his health, gives him proper training, and understands and loves him.

Calculate your dog's happiness level by adding up all of the points. Then look at the bottom of the next page to see how happy he is.

EMOTIONAL BALANCE

A happy dog has an emotional balance that leans toward the positive.

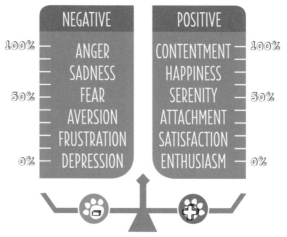

More than 90% of the time positive = 1
Between 50 and 90% of the time positive = 0
Between 0 and 50% of the time positive = -1

ENERGY LEVEL

A happy dog has a normal energy level with some natural fluctuations between low and high energy. If your dog's energy is constantly at an extremely low or extremely high level, consult your veterinarian.

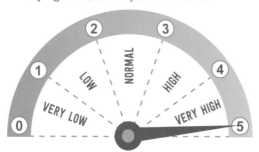

Between 2 and 3 = 1
Varying between 1 and 4 = 0
Varying between 0 and 5 = -1

SCHEDULE

A happy dog has a rich social life and doesn't spend too much time alone at home or in the yard.

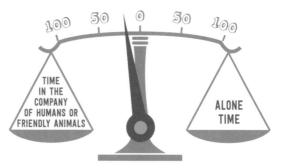

More than 75% of the time accompanied = 1
Between 50 and 75% of the time accompanied = 0
Between 0 and 50% of the time accompanied = -1

SATISFIED NEEDS

A happy dog has all of his needs met.

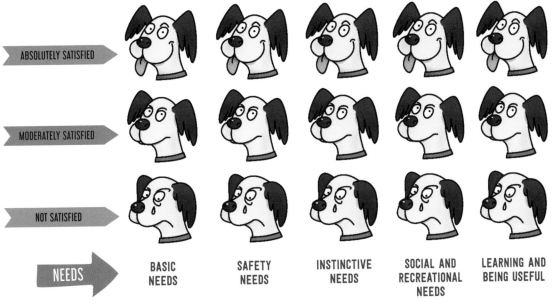

	BASIC NEEDS	SAFETY NEEDS	INSTINCTIVE NEEDS	SOCIAL AND RECREATIONAL NEEDS	LEARNING AND BEING USEFUL
ABSOLUTELY SATISFIED					
MODERATELY SATISFIED					
NOT SATISFIED					

NEEDS

5 satisfied needs = 1 • 3 or 4 satisfied needs = 0 • 1 or 2 satisfied needs = -1

STRESS METER

A happy dog is subjected to very little stress due to hunger, cold, pain, illness, noise, loneliness, boredom, punishment, insecurity, aggression, confinement, and the like.

In the green area most of the time = 1
In green and yellow areas most of the time = 0
In yellow and red areas most of the time = -1

HEALTH STATUS

A happy dog is closely monitored by a veterinarian and receives timely medical care to maintain the highest possible level of health throughout his lifetime.

In good health = 1
Being treated for illness = 0
In poor health = -1

DOG'S LEVEL OF HAPPINESS

An unhappy dog   A happy dog

 57 Is Your Dog Happy?

How to Train Your Dog

During his first year, your puppy will learn different things under your influence, under the influence of his environment, and according to his experiences. For him to become a well-adjusted and well-behaved adult, you must be a good owner and must choose a positive training approach.

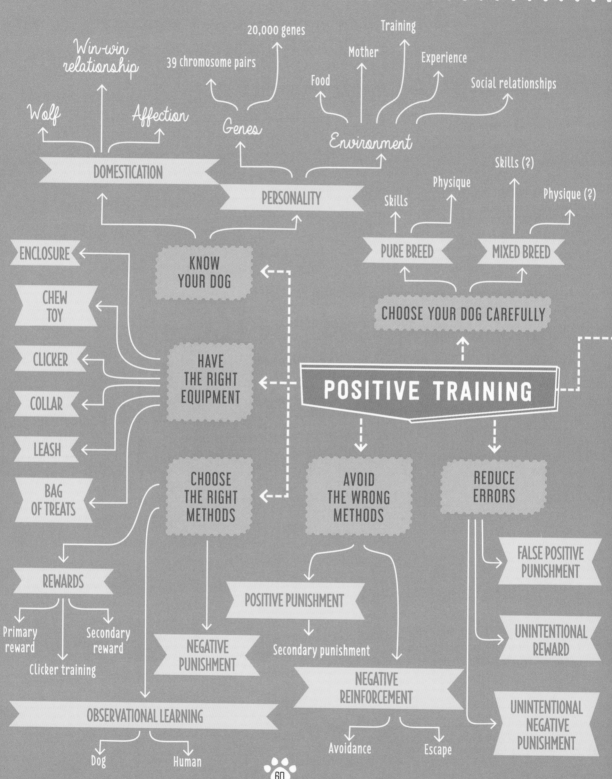

Win-win relationship

Wolf   Affection

20,000 genes

39 chromosome pairs

Training
Mother
Food
Experience
Social relationships

Genes   Environment

DOMESTICATION

PERSONALITY

Skills (?)
Physique
Skills   Physique (?)

PURE BREED   MIXED BREED

ENCLOSURE

KNOW YOUR DOG

CHEW TOY

CLICKER

COLLAR

LEASH

BAG OF TREATS

HAVE THE RIGHT EQUIPMENT

CHOOSE YOUR DOG CAREFULLY

POSITIVE TRAINING

CHOOSE THE RIGHT METHODS

AVOID THE WRONG METHODS

REDUCE ERRORS

REWARDS

Primary reward   Secondary reward

Clicker training

NEGATIVE PUNISHMENT

POSITIVE PUNISHMENT

Secondary punishment

FALSE POSITIVE PUNISHMENT

UNINTENTIONAL REWARD

OBSERVATIONAL LEARNING

NEGATIVE REINFORCEMENT

UNINTENTIONAL NEGATIVE PUNISHMENT

Dog   Human

Avoidance   Escape

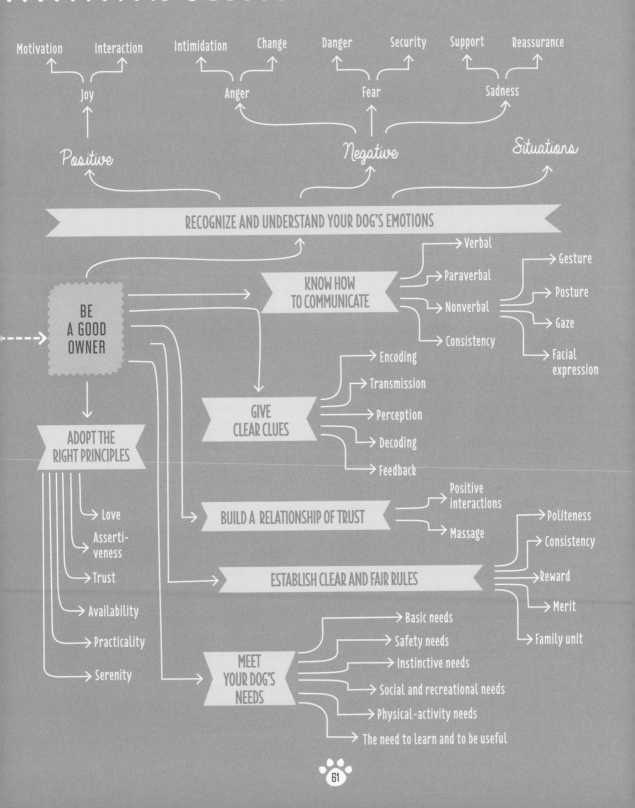

Motivation   Interaction   Intimidation   Change   Danger   Security   Support   Reassurance

Joy   Anger   Fear   Sadness

Positive   Negative   Situations

RECOGNIZE AND UNDERSTAND YOUR DOG'S EMOTIONS

KNOW HOW
TO COMMUNICATE
→ Verbal
→ Paraverbal
→ Nonverbal → Gesture
→ Posture
→ Gaze
→ Facial expression
→ Consistency

BE
A GOOD
OWNER

GIVE
CLEAR CLUES
→ Encoding
→ Transmission
→ Perception
→ Decoding
→ Feedback

ADOPT THE
RIGHT PRINCIPLES
→ Love
→ Asserti-veness
→ Trust
→ Availability
→ Practicality
→ Serenity

BUILD A RELATIONSHIP OF TRUST
→ Positive interactions
→ Massage

ESTABLISH CLEAR AND FAIR RULES
→ Politeness
→ Consistency
→ Reward
→ Merit
→ Family unit

MEET
YOUR DOG'S
NEEDS
→ Basic needs
→ Safety needs
→ Instinctive needs
→ Social and recreational needs
→ Physical-activity needs
→ The need to learn and to be useful

Choose a Dog-Friendly Training Method

To train your dog well is to consider his emotional well-being as the cornerstone of his development and future success.

A HAPPY DOG LEARNS FASTER AND BETTER

Among other forms of learning, training a puppy involves operant conditioning, i.e., associating his behavior with its consequences. If a behavior has pleasant consequences (such as a reward), the behavior tends to increase; conversely, if the consequences are unpleasant (punishment), it tends to decrease. By acting on the consequences of your puppy's behavior through reinforcement or punishment, you will guide him in his learning.

POSITIVE

INCREASES

BEHAVIOR

DECREASES

PUNISHMENT

GOOD OWNER

Happiness boosts training

GOOD TRAINER

+

POSITIVE TRAINING

HAPPY DOG

SUCCESSFUL TRAINING

Hargh!

REINFORCEMENT:

Increases the probability
of the behavior occurring

PUNISHMENT:

Decreases the probability
of the behavior occurring

POSITIVE:
the behavior
is followed
by a pleasant
stimulus

NEGATIVE:
the behavior
results in the
removal of an
unpleasant stimulus

POSITIVE:
the behavior
is followed by a
unpleasant
stimulus

NEGATIVE:
the behavior
is followed by the
withdrawal of a
pleasant
stimulus

ESCAPE

AVOIDANCE

REWARD

NEGATIVE
REINFORCEMENT

POSITIVE
PUNISHMENT

NEGATIVE
PUNISHMENT

REINFORCEMENT VERSUS PUNISHMENT: WHAT WORKS?

Regarding reinforcement, there is positive reinforcement, or reward (the master gives the dog something pleasant), and negative reinforcement (the master takes something unpleasant away from the dog). Regarding punishment, there is positive punishment (the master gives the dog something unpleasant) and negative punishment (the master takes away something pleasant from the dog).

Positive Reinforcement (Reward)

Reward, or positive reinforcement, is at the heart of positive training. For positive training to be effective, you must comply with its principles.

WHAT IS A REWARD?

A reward is **something pleasant** (petting, praise, food, playtime) that you give your dog when he meets your expectations. The best type of reward fulfills one of the dog's basic needs: food, drink, warmth, comfort, activity.

Food, in the form of treats, is the most practical, effective, and frequently used reward. It helps if the dog is a little hungry during training!

To keep your dog motivated, always carry several varieties of treats with you and be ready to reward spontaneous good behavior.

THE VET'S ADVICE

The concept of reward brings the brain's reward receptors into play, and this promotes behaviors related to the satisfaction of basic needs (eating, drinking, shelter, reproduction) or linked to a pleasant experience. The greater the need, the more motivated the dog is to satisfy it.

UNDER WHAT CIRCUMSTANCES SHOULD WE REWARD?

1 **When your dog spontaneously behaves well.** You will be surprised at what your dog can do without you having taught him. As he receives more frequent rewards for spontaneous good behavior, he will take more initiative to do well.

4 When you teach him a behavior from a greater distance.

Sit!

When I put my rear on the ground, my owner tells me to sit, and then he praises me and gives me a reward.

5 When you teach him a behavior around distractions.

WHEN TO REWARD?

The reward must be given immediately after the dog performs the desired behavior or the different stages of execution if the behavior is broken down into a series of simple acts.

2 When you teach him a new behavior.

Down!

THE DOG HEARS THE CUE

You reinforce the act of lying down.

THE DOG LIES DOWN

IMMEDIATE REWARD

3 When you teach him a behavior in a new place.

You reinforce the act of staying.

THE DOG STAYS IN THE DOWN POSITION

DEFERRED REWARD

65 Positive Reinforcement (Reward)

HOW OFTEN SHOULD I REWARD?

The frequency of rewards depends on the dog's level of learning (or progress).

1 **During the training.** Always reward your dog by saying "good" (see The Secondary Reward, page 68) and give him a treat (primary reinforcer).

Down!

> BEHAVIORAL ACQUISITION = SYSTEMATIC REWARDS

→ "Good!" ➕ 🦴

SYSTEMATIC REWARD
(secondary + primary)

2 **Once the dog understands the command.** Reward him systematically by saying "good" and giving him treats intermittently (e.g., for every third, or fifth, or tenth correct response). This helps maintain the dog's motivation.

3 **Once the command is well understood.** Reward by saying "good" intermittently and with a treat from time to time. The goal is for the dog to memorize the training over the long term.

> LONG-TERM MEMORIZATION OF BEHAVIOR = INTERMITTENT PRIMARY AND SECONDARY REWARDS

Down!

→ "Good!" ➕ 🦴
INTERMITTENT   RANDOM

> The hope of reward motivates the dog to do the right thing.

Over time, the reward must become random and essentially verbal, so that external motivation gives way to internal motivation (the satisfaction of doing well, the pleasure of learning, and the need to develop a close bond with his owner).

IMPROVE THE EFFECTIVENESS OF THE REWARD

The effectiveness of a reward depends on the dog's state of need, especially when it comes to food. The hungrier the dog is, the more motivated he will be

> I'm going to do what he asks me to do to earn that reward!

FULL DOG

HUNGRY DOG

to earn a treat, and the more effective the food rewards will be. The ideal situation, therefore, is to replace part of the dog's daily food ration, that he gets for "free," with rewards that he has "earned."

• **If you can devote yourself full-time to training your dog:** Place your dog's daily food ration in a pouch every morning. You will carry this pouch with you at all times and reward him every time he behaves well. The dog will soon understand that he must earn his daily meals. It's up to you to make him enjoy his work.

• **If you are not home all day:** A modified but equally effective solution is to divide the dog's ration into three portions: you will give the first portion (50%) to the dog at his mealtimes, the second portion (25%) as rewards for good behavior, and the third portion (25%) in a food-dispensing toy.

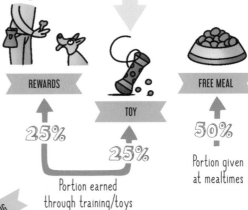

FREE MEAL 100 %

REWARDS   TOY   FREE MEAL

25%   25%   50%

Portion earned through training/toys

Portion given at mealtimes

Choose food rewards that are very small in size so you can be generous during training without the risk of overfeeding the dog.

THE VET'S ADVICE

Warning! To avoid weight gain and loss of motivation, the calories provided by the rewards should be accounted for in the dog's daily ration. Weighing or measuring out the dog's daily portion is recommended.

"Jackpots" and Secondary Rewards

The "jackpot" is your secret stash, the special treat, the training accelerator, that you use to reinforce exceptional, particularly difficult behavior (for example, if your dog stops chasing a cat to come back to Heel when you call him). As for the secondary reward, it replaces the food reward after having been repeatedly associated with it.

✚ THE VET'S ADVICE

Your dog will quickly get used to certain types, or levels, of rewards. By giving your dog an extra-special reward for extraordinary beahvior, you are sure to impress this behavior on him and encourage him to do it again.

THE JACKPOT

The jackpot must be something extra-special, a food that the dog really loves, such as a slice of sausage, a chunk of chicken, a piece of cheese—the goal is to mark the occasion in a memorable way. A dog who wins the jackpot will do anything to win it again!

To win the jackpot, I will bring you your newspaper every day!

THE SECONDARY REWARD

To be able to eventually fade out food rewards, you must set up secondary rewards. These are initially neutral stimuli that signal a reward (usually food) after being repeatedly associated with it.

To do this, you must present the secondary reward many times **before the food reward.** Once reliably combined with the food reward, the secondary reward can replace it. The most common type is verbal: "good," "yes," "good dog," or any other audible signal of your choice (such as the "click" in the clicker training; see opposite page). Thus, any praise occurring before the food reward becomes a secondary reward.

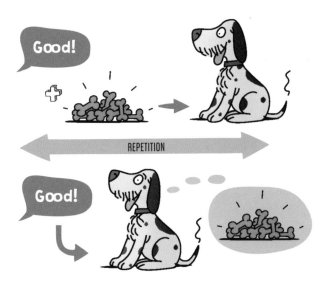

Good!

REPETITION

Good!

CLICKER TRAINING

Invented for dolphin training, clicker training is a positive, reward-based learning method. It is based on both classical conditioning (see sidebar on page 141) and operant conditioning.

Equipment

The clicker is a small box with a button that emits a special sound when pressed: the famous "click."

Rewards

The dog's training treats are combined with the click. These can be small pieces of sausage, ham, cheese, chicken, kibble, and the like, which the owner carries in a small pouch attached to his or her belt.

The Principle

The aim is to associate the click with the promise of a reward so that the click becomes a secondary reward.

To associate the click with the promise of a reward, click while holding a treat under the dog's nose and then give it to him. Then, stand at a distance, click, and give him the treat. Vary the time between the click and the reward by one to several seconds and give the treat in different ways: by hand, thrown on the floor, or on a plate.

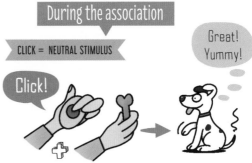

After several repetitions, the dog starts to understand the link between the click and the reward. Once this link is established, you will use the click and treat to mark desirable behavior. The dog will then learn to understand that doing what you ask of him results in a click and reward.

As with all learning, the clicks and rewards are systematic. Once the dog is reliable with a given behavior, they should become random.

Advantages of Clicker Training

It is a clear and precise method: Clicker training makes it possible to clearly establish the desired behavior. The most difficult thing is timing: if you click too early or too late, the dog will become confused about what you are rewarding him for.

It is a reliable method: Not having to use your voice reduces the risk of passing on unintended or unconscious messages or feelings through tone of voice.

It is a proactive method: The dog displays different behaviors to trigger the click and reward. This method develops the dog's thinking and intelligence. He becomes a more active participant in his training.

It is a universal method: It can be used with different learning methods, such as capturing, luring, and shaping (see pages 127, 128, 154).

Effects of Rewards

Rewards are extremely powerful behavioral motivators that enrich the dog-owner relationship and make the dog happy.

ADVANTAGES OF REWARDS

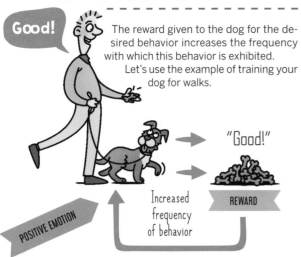

The reward given to the dog for the desired behavior increases the frequency with which this behavior is exhibited. Let's use the example of training your dog for walks.

TRUST IS ESSENTIAL FOR PROGRESS

Motivating your dog with food only works well if you have an excellent relationship of trust with the dog (see Build a Relationship of Trust, page 38).

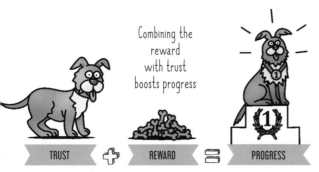

UNINTENTIONAL REWARDS

Sometimes, you unintentionally reward and thus reinforce some of your dog's undesirable behavior. This is often the case with dogs who beg for food at the dinner table or bark at the door when they are in the yard and want to come back indoors.

The example of the barking dog:

At first, you find your dog's barking helpful, so you **open the door for him every time he barks.** Without realizing it, you are giving him a systematic reward, so your dog learns to bark in front of the closed door.

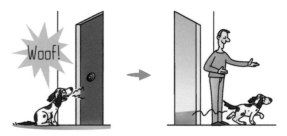

Thereafter, **you decide not to open it every time anymore.** This is an intermittent reward.

Wanting to stop your dog's annoying behavior, you ignore his barking for longer and longer periods. Very determined to get you to open the door, the dog barks louder and louder. Unfortunately, the neighbors complain. You are losing patience. When your neighbors are around and your dog starts barking his head off, you open the door. This is also an intermittent reward. By wanting to please the neighbors, you have taught your dog to bark even louder!

THE REWARD

Is effective
in the long term

Improves
the dog's
performance

Encourages
the dog
to take initiative

Works
on all dogs

Encourages the dog to be
in a good mood

Establishes
a relationship
of trust between
dog and owner

Promotes
the learning
of new
behaviors

Allows
more and
better
neural connections

Gives the dog
confidence

Generates
positive
emotions

Positive Punishment

Positive punishment is the imposition of something unpleasant on the dog as a result of undesirable behavior.

WHAT IS POSITIVE PUNISHMENT?

This type of punishment is called "positive" because it is the opposite of negative punishment, in which you take something away from the dog. It is not called "positive" because it provides the dog a sense of well-being—quite the contrary!

There are a multitude of positive punishments: tapping, turning the dog around, shaking, grabbing the scruff of the dog's neck, hitting him with a newspaper, yanking on the leash, pinching, using a shock collar, using an aggressive voice or high-intensity sound, and so on. Whatever its form, punishment causes the dog pain, discomfort, anxiety, and fear, all of which are reflected in aggression or, alternatively, inhibition, submission, and resignation. Everything you do not need in positive training!

 THE VET'S ADVICE

Both positive punishment and negative reinforcement activate a circuit in the dog's brain that allows him to deal with unpleasant situations. This encourages a fight-or-flight response. The activation of this circuit causes the release of adrenaline into the body, which prepares the dog's body for the efforts required by the fight-or-flight response.

When flight or fight proves ineffective or impossible, submission and resignation are the only possible choices in order to survive or avoid more punishment. Another circuit that inhibits fight or flight is activated, and this is a source of stress and anxiety for the dog. It triggers the release of glucocorticoids, which reduce the dog's immune defenses and may cause illness in the long term.

SECONDARY PUNISHMENT

A secondary punishment is an initially neutral stimulus that acquires a punitive association after being repeatedly associated with a positive punishment. The process is the same as that for the secondary reward. A secondary punishment is presented many times before the positive punishment. Once associated with positive punishment, secondary punishment can replace it. An example might be the verbal signal "no." According to the classical conditioning process, any stimulus occurring before the positive punishment becomes a secondary punishment. Thus, if an owner regularly tells the dog "no" before hitting the dog, then simply hearing the word "no" can cause all sorts of negative emotions in this dog.

WHY IS PUNISHMENT NOT EFFECTIVE?

An effective punishment, if such a thing really exists, should be:

1 **Immediately enforced** (in less than a second after the behavior you want to suppress). Otherwise, the dog cannot link the punishment to the bad behavior, so he will not learn to stop the behavior. Instead, the dog will adopt a kind of resignation to the punishment (acquired distress). Most times, interventions occur too late.

2 **Systematically practiced** after the behavior that you want to suppress even though there will be many times when you will not want to punish your dog (at least, I hope so!).

3 **Enforced without anger.** Unless you are a Zen practitioner, it is often difficult to stay calm when your dog has made a huge mistake. Anger is the expression of one's inability to control onself. It indicates a character flaw that is common to many of us.

4 **Enforced with sufficient intensity.** You could seriously injure a puppy or small dog by spanking him on the rear. Spanking a large, thickly coated dog may have no effect. In the worst-case scenario, you may have to take your dog to the vet urgently; in the best-case scenario, the dog will interpret your punishment as a reward.

5 **Interrupted as soon as signs of submission appear in the dog.** Failure to recognize the signs of submission results in the dog developing a state of anxiety.

FALSE POSITIVE PUNISHMENT

Some people are reluctant to really punish (no reasonable person enjoys punishing); therefore, they punish with reserve, which causes the dog to misinterpret the punishment. Unintentionally, such owners **reinforce certain behaviors while believing that they are suppressing them.**

This is the case with a dog who jumps on people and is gently pushed off or the Saint Bernard who refuses to sit down and is given a slap on the butt. The dog will consider this more as a sign of attention (and therefore a reward) than as a punishment.

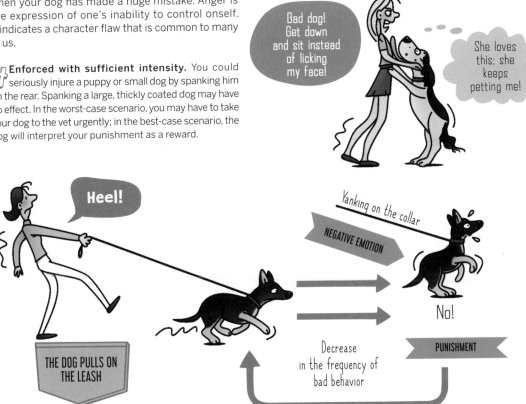

> Bad dog! Get down and sit instead of licking my face!

> She loves this; she keeps petting me!

Heel!

THE DOG PULLS ON THE LEASH

Yanking on the collar

NEGATIVE EMOTION

No!

PUNISHMENT

Decrease in the frequency of bad behavior

Effects of Positive Punishment

This method of training (which is prohibited in positive training) helps reduce the frequency with which an undesirable behavior is exhibited.

You can punish a dog who opens the cabinet to steal food, but if he is famished and has no other option, he will continue to steal to ensure his survival. (see Meet His Basic Needs, page 42).

POSITIVE PUNISHMENT MASKS THE PROBLEM WITHOUT SOLVING IT

A coercive method based on positive punishment initially provides a semblance of a response (the temporary suppression of bad behavior), but it does not eliminate the cause of the bad behavior, which the dog can then repeat.

POSITIVE PUNISHMENT AGGRAVATES THE SITUATION

Instead of improving the dog's behavior in a meaningful way, positive punishment only masks the problem and makes things worse.

1 The dog barks and growls at the sight of children. Without considering the dog's emotions (in this case, fear), the owner decides to punish him by firmly pulling on his choke collar to try to stop him from barking.

I'm afraid of children. I don't want to go near them.

THE DOG IS AFRAID OF CHILDREN

Grrr....

Woof!

Be quiet! You're hurting my ears!

Woof!

Woof!

Woof!

POSITIVE PUNISHMENT

Is ineffective
for a highly
motivated dog

Masks the problem
without solving it

Makes the dog more
cautious in
performing behaviors

"Anger is never without
reason, though it is
rarely the right reason,"
as stated by
Benjamin Franklin.

Discourages the dog
from taking initiative

Reduces
the dog's
sense of security

Breaks down the owner-dog
relationship essential
for training

Teaches
nothing

Sows the seeds
of antisocial
behaviors

Generates negative
emotions

Increases the risk of
aggression and other
behavioral problems

WRONG REASONS TO USE POSITIVE PUNISHMENT:

I'd like to give my dog a sound beating!

No!

1. Even if he keeps barking and hurting my ears?

Yes, even then.

2. But I'm tired of this dog doing everything to annoy me. Hitting him would do me good.

3. How about a little beating with a rolled-up newspaper?

No. If you want to let off steam, buy a punching bag.

No. A beating hurts, even with a newspaper.

4. Why? He'll survive a beating.

Still no!

5. Anyway, he's my dog, and I can do as I please!

In case you didn't know, dogs are not objects, but sensitive beings who are protected by law.

6. But that's the only thing they understand.

Your dog will be hurt and scared, and he won't understand anything except to be wary of you.

So, then, what is the solution?

Understand the reasons behind your dog's barking and use positive behavior modification methods. Nonviolent solutions exist and are very effective.

2 After being punished repeatedly, the dog stops barking, but his fear of children only increases. **Punishment masks the problem.**

I am right to be afraid of children because, when I see one, I get punished.

3 The dog no longer barks at the sight of the children for fear of being punished. The owner **thinks the problem is solved**, but that is not the case. When the owner approaches children, the dog, who is terrified, bites one of them without any warning (this is normal; the dog does not want to be punished).

Punishment increases the risk of aggression. To deal with the dog's fear of children, the owner should have opted for desensitization combined with counterconditioning (see pages 180-186).

I warned you!

POSITIVE PUNISHMENT SOWS THE SEEDS OF ANTISOCIAL BEHAVIOR

Punishment is the basis for physical violence, which is the breeding ground for antisocial behavior, including violence against people.

POSITIVE PUNISHMENT BREAKS DOWN THE DOG-OWNER RELATIONSHIP

A good relationship between the owner and his or her dog is essential for training. Punishment is a very powerful, and it diminishes the relationship and makes the dog unhappy.

PUNISHMENT IS A FALSE SOLUTION

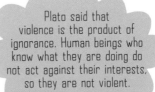

If the only educational tool you have at your disposal, out of ignorance, is punishment, it is not surprising that you see the dog only as a dominant creature who wants to control you.

Plato said that violence is the product of ignorance. Human beings who know what they are doing do not act against their interests, so they are not violent.

Anyone who only has a hammer sees all problems as nails.

Negative Punishment

This method of training consists of removing something pleasant from the dog (stopping the walk, not giving treats, ending the game, and the like).

UNDER WHAT CIRCUMSTANCES IS IT USED?

You can unintentionally suppress certain desired behaviors in your dog. For example, your dog has been roaming off-leash at the dog park, and you give him the Come cue. As soon as he comes to you, you put the dog on leash to go home and leave his playmates (negative punishment). The dog interprets it as punishment.

EFFECTS OF NEGATIVE PUNISHMENT

Negative punishment reduces the frequency with which the undesirable behavior occurs. Deprived of something that he wants, the dog will seek to obtain it by modifying his behavior. This method of punishment develops the dog's initiative by encouraging him to seek alternative behavior without fear or violence.

It must be followed by a reward when the dog adopts the desired behavior, e.g., he stops pulling on the leash or he calms down. In this way, the dog stays in a positive emotional state.

Take the example of the dog pulling on the leash during a walk. Rather than yanking on the leash forcefully (positive punishment), the owner chooses to stand still and not move forward (negative punishment). The owner then cues the dog to return to Heel position and rewards him before resuming the walk.

UNINTENTIONAL NEGATIVE PUNISHMENT

You can unintentionally suppress certain desired behaviors in your dog. This is what happens to the dog who is allowed to roam freely as soon as he responds to the Come cue. The desired behavior is that the owner puts the dog on leash (negative punishment) to go home and leave his playmates. The dog interprets it as a punishment.

Thereafter, the dog who has been "punished" may remain at a distance instead of responding properly to the Come cue. To avoid this, reward the dog for coming to you by throwing his toy a few times for him to bring back. After a few tosses of the toy, put the leash on him to go home.

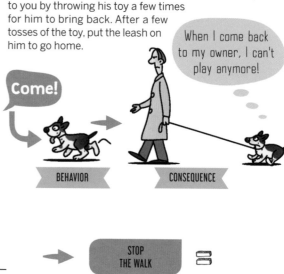

Come!

When I come back to my owner, I can't play anymore!

BEHAVIOR   CONSEQUENCE

THE DOG PULLS ON THE LEASH DURING THE WALK

STOP THE WALK

NEGATIVE PUNISHMENT

Decrease in the frequency of bad behavior

Negative Reinforcement

This form of training consists of removing something unpleasant when the dog adopts the desired behavior. It increases the frequency with which this behavior occurs. Negative reinforcement leads to two types of behavioral responses in the dog: escape (the dog avoids the unpleasant stimulus) and avoidance (the dog avoids the unpleasant stimulus by anticipating its occurrence).

ESCAPE

The dog adopts the desired behavior to avoid an unpleasant stimulus. For example, the dog wearing a choke collar (which is prohibited in positive training) walks in Heel position not for the pleasure of being close to his owner but rather to avoid having his collar pulled too tightly. It is also by escape that dogs learn to seek shelter in the yard when it rains.

AVOIDANCE

The dog adopts the desired behavior to avoid an unpleasant stimulus. Avoidance occurs after escape by learning one or more stimuli that allow him to anticipate the onset of the unpleasant stimulus. This implies that the dog remembers being punished.

Therefore, the dog walks politely on leash not for pleasure but because his neck still bears the traces of the collar wounds he's received. He knows that if the leash tightens, he will have a rough time on the walk. It is also by avoidance that a dog runs to take refuge under the table when he sees children who have already pulled his ears and tail. He hides somewhere where he knows the children cannot get to him.

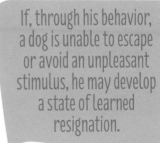

If, through his behavior, a dog is unable to escape or avoid an unpleasant stimulus, he may develop a state of learned resignation.

EXAMPLE:
LEASH WALKING IN HEEL POSITION

THE DOG IS IN HEEL POSITION, THE LEASH IS LOOSE

➡ GOOD BEHAVIOR

He receives a pleasant stimulus in the form of a food reward (primary reward) and praise (secondary reward).

THE DOG PULLS ON THE LEASH

➡ BAD BEHAVIOR

You stop, and the walk (pleasant stimulus) stops (negative punishment). When the leash loosens again (good behavior), the walk starts again.

THE DOG STOPS PULLING ON THE LEASH

➡ GOOD BEHAVIOR

You stop pulling on the collar (primary punishment) to keep the leash loose (negative reinforcement).

THE DOG PULLS ON THE LEASH

➡ BAD BEHAVIOR

The dog receives punishment (unpleasant stimulus): you yank on the leash (primary punishment) and say "no" in a low tone (secondary punishment).

Good behavior is encouraged

Bad behavior is discouraged

Good behavior is encouraged

Bad behavior is discouraged

POSITIVE EMOTIONS ➡ **NEGATIVE EMOTIONS**

Reward versus Punishment: Make the Right Choice

Your choice of reward or punishment will provoke positive or negative emotions in your dog that will influence his mood and, consequently, the way he perceives and reacts to his environment.

THE PROCESS

By positively training your dog based on reward, you set your pet up for a cycle of success. His mood is positive. He is happy, and he has self-confidence. He is proactive and constantly looking for ways to get rewards. His relationship with you is strong, and his performance is improved. Your relationship with him and understanding of him keeps improving.

Conversely, by training your dog on the basis of punishment, he enters a negative cycle of punishment avoidance, and you are setting him up for failure. His mood is negative because he thinks that there is a high probability of being punished. He is afraid. He secretes an abundance of stress hormones (adrenaline, cortisol) that are harmful to his health. His relationship with you deteriorates, and his performance level decreases.

For this reason, **rewards** and **negative punishment,** provided that the latter is associated with positive reinforcement of the desired behavior so that you always end training sessions on a positive note, **are advocated in positive training.** These methods allow the dog to progress while preserving your relationship with him. Your training should comprise about 85% reward and 15% negative punishment.

Positive punishment and **negative reinforcement,** which are vectors of negative emotions, are prohibited. If you do punish (no one is perfect), do not worry: the consequences will be less severe if the majority of your interactions are positive (see Build a Relationship of Trust, page 38).

According to a study of 364 dog owners, published in *Animal Welfare*, dogs exclusively trained using reward-based methods were significantly more obedient than those trained using punishment or a combination of rewards and punishment. Punishment is not only detrimental to the dog's well-

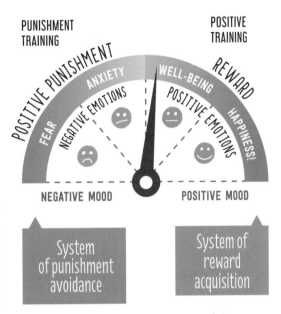

The purpose of positive training is to keep the dog in the range of positive emotions as much as possible.

being but also increases his aggressiveness and increases his risk of attacking or biting the person administering the punishment and anyone in close proximity to him.

THINK OF TRAINING AS BEING BASED ON A POINTS SYSTEM

When you start training your dog, you gain points for using positive methods that build your relatiohnship and strenghten his trust in you. When you punish your dog, you lose points, which causes your relationship to deteriorate. The only way to regain points (and, thus, trust) is by switching back to positive training right away.

Learning through Observation

Without you noticing, your puppy learns by observing other dogs as well as the humans he socializes with. These lessons are fundamental during the first months of his life, during which time he has every opportunity to observe and reproduce the behaviors of his mother and siblings.

THE ROLE MODEL

Having a "role model" (a well-behaved dog) around your new puppy makes it easier for him to learn certain behaviors, such as house-training. A puppy who goes outside with his role model and sees the other dog being rewarded for doing his business outdoors will tend to imitate the behavior to receive a reward.
A calm, polite role model can also help the puppy build his self-confidence and get over any fears he may have when out walking. A puppy who goes for walks with his owner and his role model and sees the other dog approaching and sniffing unfamiliar objects will find it easier to overcome any apprehensions about the unknown. Conversely, a stressed-out role model will cause or increase the puppy's stress.

THE SAME GOES FOR THE OWNER!

The dog also learns by observing his owner. For example, he may learn how to open doors by watching his owner press on the handle.

Aha! That's how you get out!

MOTHER IS THE BEST TEACHER

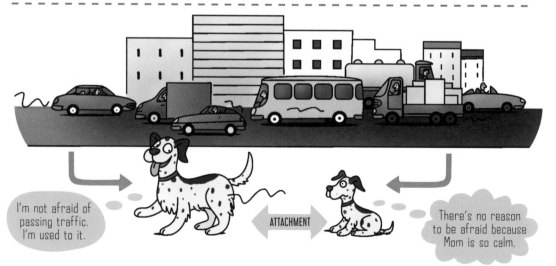

I'm not afraid of passing traffic. I'm used to it.

ATTACHMENT

There's no reason to be afraid because Mom is so calm.

Having a good companion is the best way to learn about the world.

HAVING A COMPANION

If your dog is older, and you want to adopt another dog, do so before your senior dog passes. If the older dog is well-trained, he can serve as a model for the new dog's training. It's great if your older dog wants to take the new dog under his wing because the closer the relationship between the role model and the student, the better the student's learning.

LEARNING A TRADE

Some specific behaviors may also be learned through observation. For example, this is the case with a puppy intended to be a narcotics-detection dog who is able to watch an experienced dog at work. The earlier the puppy is able to observe the behaviors that will be required of him later, the easier his future training will be. This tendency to imitate the behavior of other dogs persists throughout a dog's life, so if you have a budding agility competitor, embrace the benefits of enrolling your dog in agility classes, where he will meet others with similar pursuits.

Someday I'll be a truffle-hunting dog, too!

A Good Trainer's Equipment

A good trainer needs the right tools. Invest in high-quality equipment that is best suited to your dog's size, body type, and energy level.

EXERCISE PEN

An exercise pen will be your dog's special place. Invest in one that is sturdy and high and allows your dog enough room to be comfortable. The enclosure gives you a place where you can leave your dog alone safely; it also helps with house-training by providing an area that your dog will want to keep clean.

CHEW TOYS

Chewing is a dog's essential need. Sturdy, durable chew toys are great for teething puppies and also provide your dog with something to keep him occupied while in his enclosure. You can also give them as rewards.

OTHER TOYS

When your dog plays with you or by himself, he develops his intelligence, he is busy, he is getting physical activity, and he is expending energy in a controlled manner (see Provide Him with Physical Activity, page 52).

CLICKER

A clicker is a small box that makes a metallic "click" noise when you press it. This sound means that the dog will receive a reward (see Clicker Training, page 69).

COLLAR

Nylon collars come in all sizes and colors (can be easily matched with the dog's leash or coat) and have the advantage of being durable and washable. Leather is more elegant but more difficult to maintain.

Wider collars help cushion the pressure exerted on the dog's neck. For your dog's comfort, you must be able to fit two fingers between the collar and the dog's neck. For small dogs and dogs with heart or respiratory conditions, a harness is preferable because it prevents pressure on the neck and trachea.

LEASH

A comfortable length is about 4 to 6 feet (1.2 to 1.8 m) so that there is some slack when your dog walks properly. A leather leash is more comfortable to hold than a nylon leash, but it is less resistant to chewing.

TREAT POUCH

When attached to your belt or waistband, a treat pouch allows you to immediately reward your dog's good behavior with a portion of his daily food intake. Choose a pouch with two compartments, one for his kibble (25% of his daily food ration) and one for special "jackpot" treats (see The Jackpot, page 68).

A Good Trainer's Equipment

🐾 🐾 🐾 🐾

Part 4

Training Timeline

Your puppy's training begins at birth and continues throughout his life. Training begins at the cerebral level as the puppy associates his behavior with its consequences, acquires and organizes knowledge, and develops a representation of the world that is largely achieved during the period of primary socialization. The first year is crucial to a dog's future development. It is during this period that he discovers the world and absorbs the most information in the quickest time possible. It is akin to a human child's progress through preschool to high school, but all in the puppy's first year!

This hectic year will only go well if the puppy starts off with the training and support of his mother and siblings, and then you—his new parent and trainer—take over, guiding the puppy with love and reassurance. Your puppy needs you by his side along this essential path of discovery and learning.

The puppy's first year is divided into several overlapping periods that form a continuous, dynamic process of social maturation and constitute a specific training program. Their onset and duration are only estimates and will vary according to the breed or mix of dog and the individual dog himself.

POSITIVE TRAINING

RESPECT THE TRAINING TIMELINE

On the mother's womb

GESTATION

Alongside his mother

BIRTH– 21 DAYS

Alongside his mother

15 DAYS

Kindergarten

21 DAYS– 2 MONTHS

MOTHER'S ATTACHMENT TO HER PUPPIES

PUPPY'S ATTACHMENT TO HIS MOTHER

LEARNING TO LIVE IN SOCIETY

Discover his identity

Learn to communicate

Make friends

Animals　　Humans

Get familiar with his environment

Habituation　　Acclimatization

TRAINING TIMELINE

Elementary school

2 MONTHS– 6 MONTHS

High school

6 MONTHS– 1 YEAR

CONTINUING TO LEARN ABOUT LIFE IN SOCIETY

↓

BASIC SKILLS

→ Rules of life ←

→ Be independent ←

→ Be clean ←

→ Come when called ←

→ Walk on a leash ←

→ Be calm; know how to wait; have self-control ←

→ Accept handling ←

→ Learn basic cues ←

Clicker training   Capturing   Luring

PRACTICING WHAT HE'S LEARNED

↓

ADVANCED AND OPTIONAL TRAINING

Shaping   Capturing   Luring   Clicker training

Even if you do not get to know your puppy until you bring him home at about two months old, it is interesting to know what happened before he joined you. This will help you better understand the fundamental role of the mother and breeder in the puppy's development.

GESTATION: FIRST EMOTIONS

Your dog's life begins before he is born. It begins as soon as egg meets sperm. Gestation lasts about sixty-three days. During this period, the mother's state of mind impacts the growing fetuses. Stress and negative emotions can cause abortions, impaired growth, immune deficiencies, and learning disabilities.

The Evolution of the Puppies

• **Day 0 to Day 18 of gestation:** The eggs born from the fusion of the male and female gametes (sperm and egg) begin to undergo cell division and begin their route to the uterus.

• **Day 18 to Day 35 of gestation: This is the embryonic stage.** The embryos are implanted in the uterus. The organs begin to appear. It is during this period that the risk of birth defects is the greatest. On Day 25, the embryos' hearts begin to beat. Their heart rate is two to three times that of the mother, or between 220 and 240 beats per minute.

• **Day 35 of gestation to birth: This is the fetal stage.** Tissues and organs developed during the embryonic period grow and differentiate. The fetuses feel their first emotions. By Day 55, their bodies are completely covered with hair. The puppies' movements are perceptible by touching their mother's belly.

The Care Program

Pamper the mother. For the proper development of the puppies, the breeder must provide the mother with a quiet and safe place to rest. She should avoid all unnecessary stress: changes in schedules or habits, loud noises, being transported, strenuous activities, and the like. The breeder should show the mother affection every day, especially by stroking her tummy (puppies are sensitive to petting from Day 40 of gestation).

BIRTH TO 15 DAYS: WARM AND TOASTY WITH MOM

When the puppies are born, the mother attaches herself to her babies and provides them with the care necessary for their survival. Any separation is unbearable to her. As soon as one of her puppies moves away, she starts looking for him.

Puppy Development

• **Thermoregulation.** Unable to regulate their body temperatures themselves, the puppies crawl around in search of maternal heat or any other heat source.
• **Activity.** Puppies spend 95% of their time sleeping and the rest suckling. They are unable to stand up, so they crawl to warmly snuggle with their brothers and sisters in their mother's bosom.
• **Dentition.** The puppies' milk teeth are still hidden under the gums.
• **Feeding.** The puppies exclusively feed on breast milk. They push their muzzles into their mother's warm belly (the rooting reflex) to stimulate the milk to rise, and then they instinctively turn toward the

HYPOTHERMIA IN PUPPIES

CAUSES OF HYPOTHERMIA IN PUPPIES:
• Puppy is weak, premature, or rejected by the mother
• Incompetent mother
• Ambient temperature too low

DANGERS OF HYPOTHERMIA:
It causes poor milk digestion. It reduces swallowing reflex and appetite. If it continues, it can lead to the puppy's death.

RECOMMENDED AMBIENT TEMPERATURES FROM BIRTH ACCORDING TO AGE

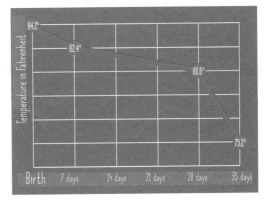

Temperature in Fahrenheit

84.2°
82.4°
80.6°
75.2°

Birth | 7 days | 14 days | 21 days | 28 days | 35 days

teats, grasp them, and suckle seven or eight times a day.

- **Sensory development.** Taste and tactile senses are well developed, but puppies see nothing, do not perceive odors (except maternal pheromones), and do not hear anything. This does not prevent them from yelping when they are cold, hungry, or far from the den. Their mother rushes in, grabs them by the scruff of the neck, and brings them back to the den.
- **Cleanliness.** After breastfeeding, their mother licks their bellies and perineal areas for them to pass urine and stool (perineal reflex). She then consumes their excrement to keep the den clean.
- **Autonomy.** Entirely dependent on their mother, puppies are not yet attached to people. In the event of death or maternal incompetence, it is possible to entrust the puppies to a substitute breastfeeding mother.

Training Program

- **A calm and safe environment.** The breeder sets up the den in a quiet, safe, and warm place and respects the puppies' sleep schedule (their growth hormones are secreted during sleep).
- **Physical contact.** Every day, the breeder pets the puppies gently, such as when they are nursing or being weighed, to promote the maturation of their tactile senses and get them used to being touched.

FROM 15 TO 21 DAYS: A MOTHER FOR LIFE

This period begins when the puppies' eyes open and ends when their hearing develops. During this time, your puppy wakes up to the world and discovers his mother.

Puppy Development

- **Thermoregulation.** The puppies remain very sensitive to sudden temperature changes. To avoid feeling cold, they sleep next to their mother and siblings. It is only around the third week that thermoregulation, linked to brain development and maturation, becomes effective.
- **Activity.** The puppies still spend more than half of their time sleeping. They can stand on all fours, even if their gait is not yet very steady. Thanks to their improved motor skills and their new sensory abilities, they leave the den to discover their environment. At the slightest fright, they come back to be reassured between their mother's paws. The more firmly

attached they are to their mother, the more their exploratory behavior will develop. Apart from their explorations, they play with their siblings and discover the objects in their environment by putting them in their mouths.

- **Dentition.** Their first milk teeth (canines) start to grow during the third week.
- **Feeding.** Most of their food is milk. Around Day 18, the puppies are able to lap, so the breeder can offer them some formula in a bowl. At the end of the third week, the mother reaches her lactation peak. To relieve her discomfort, the breeder offers the puppies a weaning mixture of puppy kibble moistened with water in bowl.
- **Cleanliness.** Puppies are not yet able to relieve themselves alone. Their mother continues to lick their bellies and perineal area to trigger the perineal reflex.
- **Sensory development.** Their eyes open to a new world. They discover their environment and can orient themselves better. They begin to hear and react to noises. At the same time, their vocal repertoire is expanding.
- **Autonomy.** They get attached to their mother. This attachment is reinforced by the mother's secretion of soothing pheromones. Any separation causes the puppies to experience a state of distress, characterized by their vocalizations and agitation. This attachment bond is essential for the puppies to identify with their species and facilitates proper socialization.

Training Program

- **Acclimatization to their environment.** To stimulate their senses and get them used to their future environment, from the third week, the breeder can set up a

bright and soundproofed wake-up room with multicolored floor mats where the puppies can have fun with toys of different colors and textures. To help them to get used to it, the breeder gradually increases the intensity and duration of the stimuli. During the puppies' rest hours, they should sleep in a calm, warm place without being disturbed.

• **Cuddling.** While next to their mother, the breeder handles and pets the puppies gently to familiarize them with his or her smell and presence.

> Cuddling is not only enjoyable, it is necessary. It promotes the puppies' attachment, increases their sense of security, and strengthens their immune systems.

FROM 3 WEEKS TO 2 MONTHS: LEARNING TO LIVE IN SOCIETY

This **period of imprinting,** or primary socialization, ends at around three months of age and is crucial in the puppies' lives. It is between four and eight weeks, on average, that the puppies are the most sensitive to their environment. After three months, the fear of the unknown dominates, and learning is more difficult.

Puppy Development

• **Thermoregulation.** The puppies are able to regulate their body temperatures. They no longer need close contact with their mother or siblings to sleep.
• **Activity.** The puppies are sleeping less. Games and interactions with their mother and siblings, and now their breeder, are becoming more and more important. Their motor coordination is improving. They walk, run, jump, fall, roll, get up, and play-fight with their mother and siblings. Through contact with them, they learn that they are dogs and learn to control themselves and "speak dog." They sniff, touch, and put objects within reach in their mouths.
• **Dentition.** The first milk teeth have already begun to appear, and by six weeks of age, the young puppies have twenty-eight teeth.

UPPER (14 teeth)

• 6 INCISORS
• 2 CANINES
• 6 PREMOLARS

LOWER (14 teeth)

• 6 INCISORS
• 2 CANINES
• 6 PREMOLARS

The eruption of their teeth makes biting painful. While playing games with their mother and siblings, they learn to control their bite intensity. They explore their environment with their mouths. They chew and sometimes shred the objects they find. It is time to offer them "approved" chew items.
• **Feeding.** Starting from the third week, the puppies are interested in food other than breast milk. Plus, the eruption of the milk teeth makes feeding painful for the mother. The mother increasingly growls and pushes away the puppies, who find something to eat elsewhere. The breeder still offers a weaning mush of puppy kibble and water, gradually reducing the amount of water. Weaning is complete around the eighth week. Puppies are then able to eat a diet of only puppy food.
• **Cleanliness.** The puppies become able to relieve themselves alone. They start by relieving themselves everywhere around the den and favor spots that have already been marked by the smell of their excrement.
• **Sensory development.** Touch, taste, smell, vision, and hearing—all of the puppy's senses are engaged. These senses are refined over time and provide them with as much information as possible about their mother, siblings, humans, environment, and any other animals around them so that their developing brains can easily memorize this information over the long term.
• **Autonomy.** They leave the den and explore their environment. They have their first fears, which can, if their mother is not there to reassure them, generate persistent fears.

Training Program

This is a senstive period for puppies. The puppies' brains, like computers, easily record and retain all of the information from their environment. All of the experiences they have, good or bad, will have a considerable and lasting impact on their temperaments and personalities. Your puppy's brain creates a database that will serve him for the rest of his life. During this period, learning takes place through contact with his mother, his brothers and sisters, his breeder, any other animal species, and the environment in which he lives. The foundation of his future behavior depends on the affection and kindness of the breeder, the quality and richness of his environment, his activities, his explorations, and his social relationships.

Each experience is imprinted in the puppies' brains and gradually builds their representation of themselves and the world.

Time spent with his mother and siblings allows your puppy to learn his identity and how to "speak dog." **The breeder gets the puppies used to their environment** (noises, lights, smells), going slowly to avoid any unnecessary fear that could impact them for a long time. The breeder can also introduce them to new people (men, women, children of all ages, including the veterinarian) and other animals in a positive context. Each new experience must be associated with positive emotions.

Beyond the imprinting period, there is no refresher course: all basic knowledge that has not been acquired during that time will be very difficult, if not impossible, to assimilate.

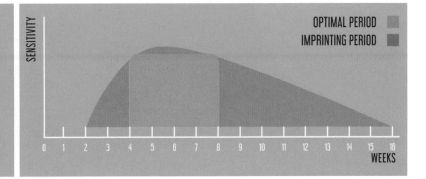

SENSITIVITY

OPTIMAL PERIOD
IMPRINTING PERIOD

0 1 2 3 4 5 6 7 8 9 10 11 12 13 14 15 16
WEEKS

From Two to Six Months

The breeder can allow you to bring your new puppy home when the puppy is around eight weeks old, no sooner. Between two and six months, your puppy continues to integrate into society, as initiated by the breeder, and starts learning the fundamental skills that are essential for his future. His physical appearance changes: he gradually loses his puppy hair, which gave him such a charming "teddy bear" look, gains weight and muscle, and develops his personality.

PUPPY DEVELOPMENT FROM 2 TO 6 MONTHS

• **Activity.** During games and activities with his owner and other dogs, your puppy learns to channel his energy. Thanks to positive training, learning new behaviors is a game he will enjoy playing. On-leash walks allow him to get used to his new environment and to meet canine friends.
• **Dentition.** Your puppy's milk teeth start to fall out around three months to give way to permanent teeth. The first to appear are the incisors, and then the canines, premolars, and molars, whose

growth ends around six months. The dog will eventually have a total of forty-two teeth:
- Upper jaw: 6 incisors + 2 canines + 8 premolars + 4 molars = 20 teeth
- Lower jaw: 6 incisors + 2 canines + 8 premolars + 6 molars = 22 teeth

Puppies have an imperative need to chew. Place inappropriate objects out of your puppy's reach and make sure that he always has something suitable to sink his teeth into, especially when he is alone.
• **Feeding.** As your puppy grows, he needs a nutritious puppy diet suitable for his age and breed. Provide four meals a day up to four months, and three meals a day up to six months. Remember to keep some of his daily portion (25%) in a treat pouch to use as rewards. To avoid digestive disorders, keep feeding your puppy the food he was eating at the breeder's or make a gradual transition over a period of several days.
• **Cleanliness.** Your puppy will get used to relieving himself on a certain surface: grass, soil, concrete—whatever you choose. Male and female puppies urinate in a squatting position. A male doesn't start lifting his leg until puberty.
• **Sensory development.** With his eyes and ears wide open, his nose upwind and on the ground, your puppy will explore his environment and enrich his sensory repertoire every day.

• **Autonomy.** After coming home with you, your puppy finds a new parent in you. With you, he can calm down when he is feeling stress, and he can continue his discovery of the world. Motivated by curiosity, he will venture farther away from you and gradually become attached to all members of the family rather than just one person. This is the prerequisite for him to become an independent adult and be able to spend time alone.

THE 2- TO 3-MONTH PROGRAM

This is the end of the imprinting, or primary socialization, period and the cornerstone of your puppy's behavioral development. Beyond this pe-

riod, there is no refresher course; all the basic social skills that he has not yet acquired will be very difficult or even impossible to obtain. Start training early and gradually so that your puppy is always relaxed and happy to have new experiences. It's the best way to ensure that your puppy is well-adjusted in preparation for his future life. Socialization is an essential prerequisite for the puppy's integration into a society of humans and other animals. A lack of socialization considerably reduces his chances of flourishing. In this sense, neglecting this learning phase can be considered a form of abuse similar to a lack of care, food, or training.

> An unsocialized dog is a powerless being, doomed to be afraid of living life.

• **Establish clear and fair everyday rules.** Start as soon as possible. The sooner the rules are in place, the easier it will be to encourage your dog's good behavior (see Establish Clear and Fair Rules, page 40).

and have fun with regularly. You can also enroll him in puppy classes.

• **Start training the fundamentals.** Begin house-training and teaching him to come when you call him (recall). Start teaching him to go to his bed, to stay in his enclosure, to eat calmly, to learn self-control, and to sit. Introduce him to wearing his collar, to walking on leash, and to being groomed. Make sure he gets used to riding in the car and visiting the vet. At the end of this period, he is becoming more independent.

• As soon as your puppy comes home, even if he does not have all of his vaccinations, **take him out for walks around the neighborhood** so that he can discover his living environment and get used to it.

• **Keep introducing him to new people** (men, women, children of all ages, people of different races, people wearing uniforms, and so on) and other animals. Each new experience must be associated with a positive emotion. Go slowly to avoid causing any unnecessary fear that could leave a lasting impression.

• **Continue his socialization with other dogs.** The ideal situation is to find your puppy a good friend—an older, well-trained dog—with whom he can play

Investing time in your puppy's early training pays off in the future.

BY 12 WEEKS OLD, A PUPPY SHOULD HAVE FACED 12 CHALLENGES:

1 Walked on different surfaces: carpets, concrete, hardwood, grass, dirt, gravel, sand, puddles, snow (if possible)

2 Played with a variety of toys of different shapes, colors, sizes, and materials (rope, hard rubber, sturdy plastic)

3 Been handled in various ways: held in someone's arms, petted on different areas of the body, brushed or combed, wiped down, had his ears and eyes cleaned, nails clipped, teeth brushed

4 Explored all around the home: living room, bedroom, up and down the stairs, bathroom, kitchen, basement, garage, backyard

5 Heard a number of domestic noises: washing machine, dishwasher, hair dryer, vacuum, television, radio, baby crying, phone ringing

6 Smelled many different scents: human and animal body odors, perfumes, flowers, odors, household products

7 Tasted a variety of foods: cheese, safe fruits (e.g., bananas and apples), meat (beef, pork, lamb, chicken, turkey, ham), starchy foods (pasta, rice), safe vegetables (zucchini, green beans, broccoli), treats (salami, hot dogs)

8 Met various types of people: men and women, children and teenagers, senior citizens, people in wheelchairs, people who walk with canes, the veterinarian, the mail carrier

9 Been in contact with other animal species: cats, rabbits, birds, farm animals

10 Visited different places: the park, shopping mall, outdoor cafe, kids' school, sporting events

11 Been exposed to street noises: road traffic (cars, trucks, scooters, motorcycles), car horns, ambulance and police sirens

12 Taken different modes of transport: car, subway, train, elevator, escalator

> 7:00: Good morning! Petting and cuddling.

> 7:15: Potty walk.

> 7:30: Breakfast.

> 8:00: Games in the house and yard, supervised exploration, and brief training session.

> 9:00: Quiet time with chew toys.

> 10:30: Walk for potty, socialization, and exercise.

> 11:00: Games in the house and yard, supervised exploration, and brief training session.

> 12:00: Lunch.

> 12:30: Walk for potty, socialization, and exercise.

> 1:00: Games in the house and yard, supervised exploration, and training session.

> 2:00: Quiet time with chew toys.

> 3:30: Walk for potty, socialization, and exercise.

> 4:00: Games in the house and yard, supervised exploration, and training session.

> 4:30: Snack.

> 5:00: Trip to the park for a potty walk, meeting/playing with other dogs, and exploration.

> 5:30: Rest in the park with chew toys.

> 7:00: Potty walk.

> 7:15: Games in the house and yard, supervised exploration, and training session.

> 8:00: Dinner.

> 8:30: Potty walk.

> 8:45: Quiet time, television, and cuddles with the whole family.

> 10:30: Potty walk.

> 10:45: Bedtime! Puppy goes into his enclosure for the night with some chew toys.

Zzzz

THE 3- TO 6- MONTH PROGRAM

The curiosity of the puppy's previous life stage is followed by a certain distrust of the unknown.

• To maintain and build upon his achievements, **keep taking him** to all kinds of places, let him regularly spend time with a well-behaved dog who can set an example for him, and keep up his relationships with the people around him.

• **Continue the training that you started at two months.** Your puppy must be able to stay alone in his enclosure, eat calmly, show self-control, come when called, sit on cue, and heel on leash. He should be accustomed to car rides, visits to the vet, and basic grooming. Teach him to give up his toy, go to his bed, and stop undesirable behaviors.

• **Continue encouraging his independence.**

• **Keep strengthening your relationship with your dog** to cement the bond that unites you. You will need a strong bond, especially throughout his puberty period.

Socialization

Perfect His Canine Communication Skills 104
Acclimate Him to His Environment 106
Introduce Him to People 110
Introduce Him to Other Animals 112

Perfect His Canine Communication Skills

After your puppy leaves his mother and siblings, around the age of two months, you must keep introducing him to other dogs, such as at the park or at puppy classes, so that he can improve his self-control (bite, play, and the like) and his "dog speak."

case of an orphaned newborn puppy raised by a human or a cat, without his mother and siblings. This puppy will identify himself as a human or a cat and will consider fellow dogs as another species.

TEACH HIM THAT HE IS A DOG

Repeated contact with other dogs is essential for your puppy's development, especially up to twelve weeks old. There must be other dogs in his life. Consider the

A dog's identity determines his future social relationships.

IMPRINTING

HUMAN

CAT

DOG

PUPPY CLASSES

As soon as you have your puppy, enroll him in puppy classes so he can continue to play with his peers and improve his communication with other dogs.

GOING ON WALKS

If, during a walk, your puppy expresses a desire to approach another dog, make sure that the other dog is dog-friendly before letting your puppy approach.

DO NOT FORCE IT!

If your puppy does not want to play with a dog he doesn't know, do not force him. He has the right to choose his playmates.

Acclimate Him to His Environment

Before three months old, the puppy has a high habituation capacity. This process is all the more effective when the dog is young and the stimulus (i.e., what you are trying to get him used to) is presented often, initially with a low intensity, and then increases. This process is naturally implemented when a puppy has to get used to a new environment.

INCREASE THE STIMULI

In addition to the wake-up room, give your puppy access to the rest of the house and the yard. Start taking him out onto the street and to the places he will eventually frequent so that he can discover and get used to his living environment by creating a kind of sensory register for reference. The richer his environment will be in terms of various stimuli (tactile, gustatory, auditory, olfactory, and visual), the better will be his ability to adapt in the future.

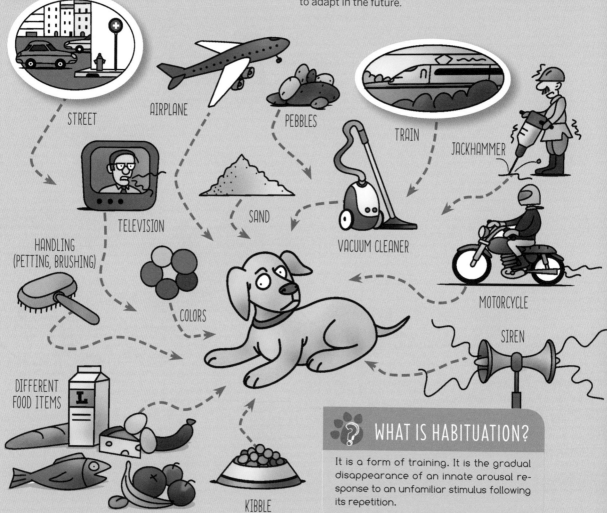

STREET

AIRPLANE

PEBBLES

TRAIN

JACKHAMMER

TELEVISION

SAND

VACUUM CLEANER

HANDLING (PETTING, BRUSHING)

COLORS

MOTORCYCLE

SIREN

DIFFERENT FOOD ITEMS

KIBBLE

WHAT IS HABITUATION?

It is a form of training. It is the gradual disappearance of an innate arousal response to an unfamiliar stimulus following its repetition.

HOW DO YOU ACHIEVE HABITUATION?

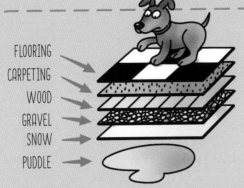

FLOORING
CARPETING
WOOD
GRAVEL
SNOW
PUDDLE

1 Introduce your puppy to the different surfaces he will walk on.

2 Walk your puppy in different places so that he can encounter the sounds, sights, scents, and tactile stimuli that he will encounter in the future. Make these walks enjoyable to him by giving him treats or playing with him as you walk.

3 Take different modes of public transport: train, boat, taxi, bus, subway, and the like.

4 Take him into an elevator. Teach him to walk up and down stairs. Ride an escalator if possible.

5 Take him to the groomer and veterinarian. Give him plenty of praise and treats during these visits.

6 If you want your puppy to wear a muzzle, put a treat inside it so putting it on will be a positive experience (see The Collar, Muzzle, and Harness, page 135).

GENERATE POSITIVE EMOTIONS

To make a good impression on your puppy, all of his new experiences must generate positive emotions; therefore, they must be associated with things that he really enjoys, like a toy or treats. To help him in his discoveries, bring along your puppy's well-socialized "role model" dog friend as a guide and tutor and to help him deal with any apprehension (see Learning through Observation, page 82).

AVOID NEGATIVE EMOTIONS

Gradually increase the intensity and duration of the stimuli that you introduce your puppy to. If you want him to discover your town's shopping area, do not take him there for the first time on a Saturday afternoon! Avoid all frightening situations that could cause persistent phobias (fireworks, sirens, etc.). Always be relaxed so you do not convey any apprehension to your puppy (see Learning through Observation, page 82).

THE VET'S ADVICE

For the imprinting period to be effective, your puppy must always be cheerful and lively. If he is uncomfortable, nervous, frightened, excited, or aggressive, talk to your vet.

AVOID SENSITIZATION AND PHOBIAS

Sensitization is the opposite process of habituation. It occurs when the dog does not confront the object of his fear over time and thus cannot gather sufficient information about its real characteristics in order to realize that it is not dangerous or threatening. Through repetition, the stimulus triggers an ever-increasing arousal response, which can evolve into a phobia (an exaggerated reaction of fear in relation to the situation). The dog is ill-adapted to his environment.

Surround your puppy with affection so that he will see you as a parent who provides him with the necessary security to continue his discovery of the world. Proceed with care so that you avoid sensitizing him to certain environmental stimuli and thus developing phobias to these stimuli. Sensitization to fireworks is one of the most common types of sensitization.

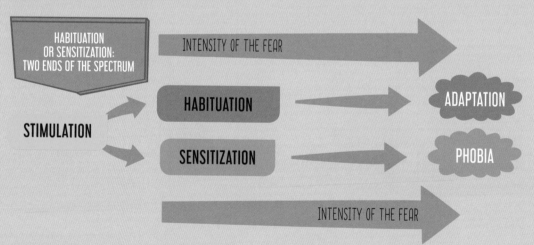

WHAT ARE THE CONSEQUENCES FOR FUTURE DEVELOPMENT?

Depending on the quality of your puppy's sensory register, or sensory memory, a kind of database established during the imprinting period, he will have more or less intense reactions to the varied stimuli he will encounter in future.

1 Your puppy goes outside, hears a noise, and searches his sensory memory.

2 If he is familiar with the noise, he does not react, or reacts only slightly.

3 If the noise is unknown to him, he will experience an arousal response.

Puppies with more extensive sensory registers will be calmer and more relaxed during their outings once the imprinting period has passed.

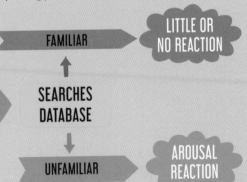

STIMULUS → **SENSORY ORGANS** → SENSORY REGISTER → **SEARCHES DATABASE**

FAMILIAR → **LITTLE OR NO REACTION**

UNFAMILIAR → **AROUSAL REACTION**

Introduce Him to People

To have a dog who is comfortable in all circumstances, you must not only provide a rich environment that allows him to explore and act independently but also encourage him to create links with others (humans and animals). To become familiar with the human species, the puppy needs contact with his breeder and different people.

ACT QUICKLY!

From three to five weeks old, a puppy is attracted to all individuals, regardless of species. This attraction allows him to create strong bonds of friendship.

From the fifth week, he begins to develop fear of the unknown and is less attracted to what is unfamiliar. The puppy is not as interested in new species and begins to become suspicious of them.

After the twelfth week, fear of the unknown dominates, and socialization is more difficult. The puppy becomes wary of species not previously recorded as friends in his memory database. His response may be to turn away from them and flee. Therefore, the optimal time for these meetings to take place is between the fourth and eighth weeks.

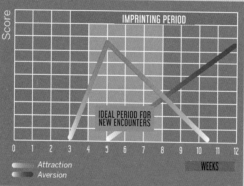

IDEAL TIME FOR NEW ENCOUNTERS

Score

IMPRINTING PERIOD

IDEAL PERIOD FOR
NEW ENCOUNTERS

0 1 2 3 4 5 6 7 8 9 10 11 12

WEEKS

Attraction
Aversion

LET HIM MEET HUMANS OF ALL KINDS

Give your puppy the opportunity to meet people of all kinds in a positive context, because friendship with humans is not something that dogs generalize.

DIFFERENT KINDS OF PEOPLE

MOTORCYCLIST

SENIOR CITIZEN

CHILDREN

DELIVERY PERSON

BABY

SOMEONE WITH A HAT AND/OR GLASSES

DIFFERENT RACES

PERSON IN WHEELCHAIR

Hello!

Let your puppy approach new people at his own pace, if and when he wants to. Associate the new encounters with positive reinforcement.

Sausage!

Make sure that the meetings are varied but always friendly and positive.

THE ISSUE WITH CHILDREN

A three-month-old puppy who has never seen children in his life will have a normal reaction of mistrust, even fear (which will result in running away, "freezing" in place, or even aggressive behavior), during their first encounter. And if it goes wrong (if, for example, the child pulls his tail), he may definitively classify children as a dangerous species, not to be socialized with at all!

HOW TO SAY HELLO TO A PUPPY WHILE RESPECTING CANINE ETIQUETTE

- Stand at the puppy's side.
- Let him come closer to you and sniff you.
- Crouch to get down to his level.

- Gently pet him on his sides and back.
- Speak to him in a low, affectionate voice.
- Give him a treat to thank him for spending time with you.

Introduce Him to Other Animals

MEDIUM

Introduce your puppy to other animal species in the same way you introduce him to humans.

THE EXAMPLE OF HERDING DOGS

To become good livestock protectors, Great Pyrenees puppies live with their mothers among the sheep herds from an early age. In this way, sheep become friends that they will defend against predators when they become adults.

❓ AS SOON AS POSSIBLE

The lessons learned during the imprinting period form the foundation for your puppy's future behavior. Start as early and gradually as possible so that he is always relaxed and happy to have new experiences. It's the best way to ensure that your puppy is well-adjusted in preparation for his future life.

Time goes by quickly! Take advantage of this precious time to correctly train your dog; it will be much more difficult later.

MEETING YOUR ADULT CAT

If your cat has never seen a dog before, she will not be happy and will view it as an inconvenience when a small ball of fur arrives in her territory.

1 To reassure your cat, apply a spray containing cat facial pheromones to the puppy's face and sides.

2 Before the first meeting, take your puppy for a long walk so he is tired, trim the cat's claws (you never know!), and feed them both.

3 For their first meeting, place your puppy in his enclosure and let the cat into the room. This will allow your cat to safely approach the puppy and get used to his smell.

4 When they meet in an open space, be sure the cat has an escape route or a place to perch at a height to be safe. The first contact can be a little rough, with the cat arching her back, but the puppy will quickly understand not to push the cat's boundaries.

5 Be careful; friendship between dogs and cats is very selective. If your puppy has become friends with your cat, he may not like your friend's cat or the the neighborhood cats who come and annoy him in his own territory.

DOG AND CAT: TWO DIFFERENT LANGUAGES

Dogs and cats do not have the same communication modes, which leads to frequent misunderstandings.

• When a cat is being chased, she rolls onto her side and exposes her belly to gain an advantage during an attack, while a dog exposes his belly in an expression of submission and peace.

• When a cat raises her paws, it is to keep an opponent at a distance, whereas a dog is indicating that he wants to play.

• When a dog wags his tail, he usually wants to to play, while a cat expresses anger by wagging her tail.

113 Introduce Him to Other Animals

Basic Skills

Independence 116

House-Training 118

Coming When Called (Recall) 120

Going to His Bed and Staying There 121

Enclosure Training 124

Sit and Down 126

Stay 130

Eating Calmly 131

Self-Control 133

The Collar, Muzzle, and Harness 135

Walking on Leash 136

Nail Clipping and Other Grooming 140

Visiting the Veterinarian 141

Riding in the Car 142

Giving Up a Toy 143

Interrupting Behavior 144

Look at Me 145

Independence

MEDIUM

Welcoming an eight-week-old puppy who has just left his mother means opening your heart and arms to him. It is important that he finds a new parent in you: someone who takes care of him, reassures him, and guides him in his training and discovery of the world. The puppy's mother starts tactfully and gently teaching him to become independent, and you must continue this training.

THE MAIN PRINCIPLES

1 **Encourage attachment to all family members** so that the puppy is not dependent on one person. The whole family must take care of him (feed him, play with him, take him out, train him, and reassure him).

2 **Do not worry about him** constantly when you are at home.

Do you want to play?

3 **While walking,** allow him to meet and play with other dogs.

4 **If you live alone** with your dog, choose a caretaker who will look after him when you can't and with whom he can develop emotional bonds.

Do you want to be Bobby's godfather?

5 Do not respond freely to his requests. Teach your puppy to ask for something politely by sitting for petting or a treat (see Establish Clear and Fair Rules, page 40).

Can I please have a hug?

6 Start with short absences, and then gradually increase their duration.

Home already?

7 Teach him to go to his bed or enclosure (see pages 121 and 124).

8 After walks or playtime, give your puppy some quiet time alone, as he will be tired and want to sleep.

9 Make sure that your puppy has something safe to chew on in your absence.

10 Avoid departure and return rituals. Go out and come back calmly without big displays of emotion.

?

11 If you have to be away all day, entrust him to a dog sitter.

🐾➕ THE VET'S ADVICE

There are collars infused with pheromones (reassuring scents) that encourage independent behavior.

House-Training

MEDIUM

House-training should begin as soon as your puppy comes home and requires frequent outings at regular times. By six months old, most puppies are toilet-trained; some take more or less time to become reliable. This training uses the puppy's natural defecation and urination reflexes.

Always take him out to the same place, so he can find the "good smells" he left behind.

THE BEST TIMES TO TAKE A PUPPY OUT

1 After eating or drinking. A full stomach naturally triggers the puppy's urination and defecation reflexes.

MAX

2 Upon waking up.

3 After playing.

DURING THE NIGHT

At night, if he wakes up or if he is about to do his business (walking around in circles, sniffing the ground), take him outside to the spot where you want him to relieve himself.

I have to go!

HOW MANY OUTINGS PER DAY?

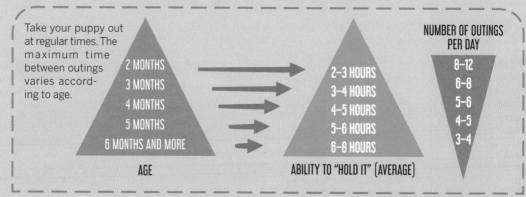

Take your puppy out at regular times. The maximum time between outings varies according to age.

AGE	ABILITY TO "HOLD IT" (AVERAGE)	NUMBER OF OUTINGS PER DAY
2 MONTHS	2–3 HOURS	8–12
3 MONTHS	3–4 HOURS	6–8
4 MONTHS	4–5 HOURS	5–6
5 MONTHS	5–6 HOURS	4–5
6 MONTHS AND MORE	6–8 HOURS	3–4

✚ THE VET'S ADVICE

Do not wait until all of your puppy's vaccinations are complete to take him out in public. It is important for him to become familar with his environment from an early age.

IN THE EVENT OF AN ACCIDENT

If your dog has relieved himself in an unsuitable place, do not punish him and do not put his nose in it. Clean it with diluted white vinegar when he is not around.

TEACH HIM TO DO HIS BUSINESS ON WALKS

1 As soon as the puppy has finished his meal, take him out for a walk.

2 When he starts circling and sniffing (characteristic signs of the urge to go), move him to the curbside to relieve himself.

3 As he relieves himself, say "go potty" or another phrase to teach him this verbal cue.

Go potty!

When he tells me to "go potty," I do my business.

4 As soon as he is finished, reward him with petting, praise, or a treat. Be aware, however, that the satisfaction of relieving himself is in itself a positive reinforcement.

5 After repeated outings of taking him for walks and leading him to the curbside, he will develop the conditioned reflex of wanting to relieve himself.

Warning! If you teach your puppy to relieve himself in the house on newspapers, it will be very difficult for you to teach him to do his business outdoors.

Out of courtesy and to avoid fines, do not forget to pick up after your dog!

Coming When Called (Recall)

EASY

Recall training is one of the most basic skills. Training should begin soon after the puppy's arrival so that he starts to build a loving relationship with you right away.

Never punish your dog when he comes to you.

1 **Crouch down,** tap your thighs, and spread your arms while saying your puppy's name in a playful voice, followed by the cue "come."

Max, come!

3 **Gradually increase the degree of difficulty:** from farther and farther away and with more and more distractions. The most important thing is to put the dog in a position to succeed.

Max, here!

2 As soon as he comes to you, even if it's not immediate, **praise him by saying** "good!" Reward him with a treat and pet him.

Practice many times a day, gradually reducing the frequency of rewards. Initially, for safety reasons, start in an enclosed yard or have your dog on a long line.

4 Combine the verbal cue "come" with another audible signal, such as a whistle, to be able to call your dog back from a long distance.

Good!

Tweeet!

THE VET'S ADVICE

Avoid calling your dog to you to put his leash on immediately; the dog will view this as a negative punishment (see Negative Punishment, page 78).

As with all training, the reward is consistent at the beginning and then becomes random.

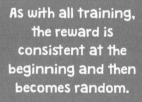

Going to His Bed and Staying There

EASY
1

MEDIUM
1 1

To feel safe, your dog needs a place to sleep (bed, crate, rug, mat) where he can have some alone time and know he will not be disturbed. This is his private domain. To be a true refuge, it must be located away from high-traffic areas of the house, in a quiet and draft-free place.

1 Place his bedding in a quiet and comfortable place in the home with treat-dispensing toys and safe chew objects.

3 Once he is lying in his bed, praise him by saying "good," pet him, and give him a treat.

Good!

I only get this great stuff in bed.

4 Repeat several times until he goes into his bed on his own to play with toys, chew, or rest.

Good!

5 Introduce the verbal cue "go to your bed" and the gesture of pointing to the bed just before he goes to lie down there. Soon, all you will have to do is point to his bed to get him to go there on his own.

Shhh... Good night!

2 Attract him to his bed with a treat.

WITH THE CLICKER

To teach him how to go to his bed, you can also capture his behavior using the clicker. The dog lies spontaneously in his bed. Just as he does this, click and give them a treat.

Click!

Go to your bed!

Then, introduce the verbal cue "go to your bed" and point to the bed as he is going to lie down in his bed.

TEACH HIM TO STAY IN HIS BED IN YOUR PRESENCE

1 Several times during the day, for example, when you are watching television or reading the newspaper, tell your dog to go to his bed and reward them for doing so.

Go to your bed!

2 If he gets up, give him the verbal cue again and, once he is in his bed, reward him so he learns to stay there for longer periods.

TEACH HIM TO STAY IN HIS BED IN YOUR ABSENCE

1 Once he knows the cue "go to your bed" well, send him to his bed (see page 121).

Go to your bed!

2 While he is in his bed resting or busy playing with his toys, **leave the room,** keeping the door open.

3 **Come back after five seconds.** If he is lying in his bed, do not say anything. Otherwise, send him back to his bed and repeat step 1. **Progressively increase the duration** of your absence: ten, then twenty, then forty seconds and then one minute, two minutes, four minutes, and so on.

Go to your bed!

4 Repeat steps 1, 2, and 3 with the door ajar and then closed.

DEALING WITH ISSUES

1 If your puppy has trouble sleeping alone, move his bed into your room.

2 First, teach him to be alone for a while during the day. Gradually, transition him to sleeping alone at night in his bed or in an enclosure outside your room.

? DON'T WORRY ABOUT IT!

Leaving your dog alone with treat-filled toys and safe chew objects for a few hours is like leaving your child alone in his or her room with the video game console! It's not as good as physical activity, but it's not a problem if you have to do it from time to time.

Nevertheless, a dog needs a certain amount of daily activity (see Provide Physical Activity, page 52). Rather than leaving your dog alone all day, it is always better to entrust his care to a dog daycare center or a dog sitter.

+ THE VET'S ADVICE

The more independent your dog is, the easier it is for him to stay alone in his bed. Collars infused with pheromones encourage autonomous behavior, but, in some cases, the dog's emotional reaction (fear, anger, sadness) is such that only drugs prescribed by the veterinarian will help him calm down.

Enclosure Training

When you cannot monitor him, it is a good idea to secure your young puppy somewhere safe, such as in a puppy-proofed room behind a barrier, or a large puppy enclosure (exercise pen) rather than leaving him free to roam around the house, risking dangerous or destructive behavior. We use the example of the exercise pen here.

HOW TO USE THE PUPPY ENCLOSURE

• Buy a large enclosure that will accommodate his adult size.
• Never use the enclosure as a punishment.
• Never put the puppy in the enclosure for more than two hours. He needs exercise and interaction! If you are gone for long periods of time, a dog sitter or dog daycare center are preferable solutions.
• Normally, a puppy wants to keep his area clean and will not relieve himself in his enclosure. If he could not hold it and had an accident, it is because you left him in the enclosure for too long.
• Never leave the puppy without a durable chew toy.
• Never disturb the puppy when he is in his enclosure.

TEACH HIM TO GO TO HIS ENCLOSURE

1 **Place the enclosure in a quiet**, comfortable room in the house with a bed or mat, toys, and chew objects.

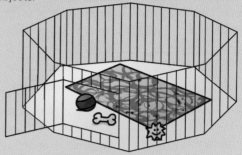

2 **Lure your dog** to the enclosure with a treat.

THE VET'S ADVICE

Your puppy should only be enclosed in his pen or area when you cannot supervise him. The rest of the time, the door should be open so that the area is freely accessible to him. As your puppy grows up and becomes reliably house-trained and well-behaved in the house, you can use the enclosure as a sleeping area and quiet place for him, but confinement in your absence will no longer be necessary.

3 When your puppy is in the exercise pen, praise him by saying "good!" and give him a treat. Leave the door open. **Repeat** the process several times until he returns to his enclosure on his own to play with his toys, chew, or rest.

"Good!"

4 Next, introduce a verbal cue, such as "go to your place" and gesture (point to the pen) before he goes inside it. Then, all you will have to do is point your finger at his pen, and he will go inside on his own.

Go to your place!

Several times a day, send him to his enclosure and reward him, still keeping the pen door open.

TEACH HIM TO STAY IN THE CLOSED PEN IN YOUR PRESENCE

1 Once he is familiar with the verbal cue and hand signal, send him to his pen and then **close the door** of the pen while he eats a few treats or chews on his toys.

2 Gradually increase the duration of how long you keep the door closed (ten, then twenty, then forty seconds and then one minute, two minutes, four minutes, and so on) while you remain nearby **so that he can get used to being in the pen with the door closed.**

TEACH HIM HOW TO STAY IN THE CLOSED PEN IN YOUR ABSENCE

Repeat the previous steps but leave the room, first with the door open, then half-opened, and then closed. When you come back into the room, if he is calm, open the door; if not, ignore him until he calms down and then open the door.

Sit and Down

Two different techniques—capturing and luring—work when teaching Sit and Down. Capturing involves waiting for the behavior to occur and then rewarding the puppy. Luring, as its name suggests, involves guiding the dog into the behavior with a lure (such as a treat) and then rewarding him.

1 **The dog sits spontaneously.** Just as his rear end hits the ground, say "good!" and give him a treat.

Good!

Sit!

Next, introduce the verbal cue "sit" combined with a hand signal as he sits.

2 **The dog lies down spontaneously.** Just as his body hits the ground, say "good!" and give him a treat.

Good!

Down!

Then, introduce the verbal cue "down" and a hand signal as he lies down.

Once he has associated the cues with the behaviors, stop rewarding the spontaneous behaviors and reward only those correct responses to your verbal or visual cues.

THE VET'S ADVICE

The Sit and Down cues are only two classic examples. The number of cues you can teach your dog is limited only by your imagination: Sit Pretty, Play Dead, Roll Over, Shake Paw, and many more.

> Capturing reinforces behaviors that your dog does naturally.

BEHAVIOR CAPTURING

This technique is used without any force—as this is not allowed in positive training—and allows the dog to take the initiative. You are simply encouraging your dog to repeat a natural behavior that you value.

It allows him to learn simple behaviors by rewarding them and associating them with verbal cues and hand signals. It is about rewarding a desired behavior that the dog naturally does on his own: sitting, lying down, relieving himself, coming to you, barking, taking an object in his mouth, etc. With this technique, the most difficult thing is to mark (with the verbal cue and hand signal) and reward the desired behavior at the right time. This extremely simple learning technique works well for teaching basic cues; it can also be a great source of pride for children, as it allows them to participate in their dogs' training.

CAPTURING WITH THE CLICKER

If you are precise with the timing of your clicks and rewards, the clicker can be very effective for capturing (see Clicker Training, page 69).

1 **The dog sits spontaneously.** Just as his rear hits the floor, click and give him a treat. Next, introduce the verbal cue "sit" with a hand signal.

2 **The dog lies down spontaneously.** Just as his body hits the floor, click and give him a treat. Next, introduce the verbal cue "down" with a hand signal.

> **Each reward reinforces the link between the cue (verbal and hand signal) and the behavior. As with all training, the treats are consistent at first, and then once the dog is reliably performing the behavior, the rewards become random.**

TEACH SIT WITH LURING

1 **Show a treat to your dog.** Hold the treat first in front of his nose, then move it up to his eye level, and then over his head.

2 To follow the treat with his eyes, the dog will his naturally raise his head and lower his rear end until he is **in a sitting position**.

3 **Just as he sits,** praise him by saying "good!" and give him the treat. Then, introduce the verbal cue "sit" combined with a hand signal just before he sits.

Good!

TEACH DOWN WITH LURING

For this training, the dog must already know the Sit cue.

1 Start with steps 1 and 2 for Sit to get your dog in a Sit position. Once he is sitting, move the treat down and then toward you so he follows it and lies down.

2 As soon as he is fully down, say "good!" and give him the treat. Then, introduce the verbal cue "down" combined with a hand signal as he starts to lie down.

"Good!"

Over time, the dog will no longer need to follow the treat.

? LURING BEHAVIOR

The main disadvantage of the capturing technique is that it may take a long time to achieve the desired behavior.

Luring is an effective method for teaching not only body positions such as lying down and sitting but also movements such as rolling, turning left, turning right, and heeling beside you that the dog might not spontaneously perform as readily.

This technique involves presenting the dog with a lure (a treat) that you hold in your hand and use to guide the dog into a particular behavior. You teach your dog by praising him and giving him the lure (treat) as a reward. Once he understands what behavior you want, pair it with a verbal cue and hand signal before requesting the behavior.

TEACH SIT AND DOWN WITH LURING AND THE CLICKER

1 Show the treat to the dog and move it from in front of his nose to his eye level to above his head.

2 To follow the treat with his eyes as it moves over his head, the dog will raise his head and lower his rear until he is in a sitting position. Click at this precise moment and give him the treat.

Click!

Next, introduce the verbal command "sit" and a hand signal.

3 Once the dog is in a sitting position, move the treat to the ground and toward you until he lies down. Click at that precise moment and give him the treat.

Click!

Next, introduce the verbal cue "down" and a hand signal.

As with all training methods, the click and the reward are consistent at first, and as soon as the dog reliably performs the behavior, the rewards become random.

Stay

The Stay cue is essential in a dog's daily life. It allows you to keep your dog waiting politely when you talk to friends on the street, when you open your front door, or when you serve him his food. For this training, the dog must know the Sit cue.

3 Gradually increase the duration for which you expect your dog to stay, and then increase your distance from him. To do this, first make eye contact with him and then look away. Dogs are a little like children: they often do as they please when the teacher's back is turned. If he stays in position, come back to him, tell him "good!", and give him a treat. The dog needs to learn that he must remain still to receive a reward.

Sit!

1 With your dog facing you, give him the Sit cue. Once he is sitting, tell him "stay" and raise your palm vertically, facing him.

Don't move!

Good!

2–3 SECONDS

2 Wait a few seconds and, if he stays in the Sit, say "good!" and give him a treat. Otherwise, repeat step 1.

Good!

Each reward reinforces the link between the cue (verbal cue and hand signal) and the behavior. As with all training, initially the praise and the treats are consistent; once the dog understands and responds reliably to the cue, the rewards become random.

Eating Calmly

Resource-guarding behavior is natural in dogs. The purpose of this training is to make your dog understand that our presence does not threaten his food resources in any way; in fact, quite the contrary.

1 **Feed meals on a regular schedule** and always in the same place. Cue your dog to sit (see Sit and Down, page 126).

Sit!

stay!

2 **Once he sits,** tell him to stay as you put down his bowl with only a handful of food in it.

3 **If he gets up,** take the bowl away, cue him to sit, and start again.

Sit!

4 Once the bowl is in place and the dog is sitting still, wait a few seconds and then give him the verbal cue "eat" as you point at his bowl. Gradually increase the interval between putting the bowl down and giving him the cue to eat.

Eat!

5 Once the bowl is empty, your dog will look at you in the hope of getting a refill.

Again!

✚ THE VET'S ADVICE

Offering your dog some of his food as a reward after he performs a requested behavior allows you to put yourself in a position of positive leadership.

6 Cue him to sit and stay, put a handful of food in his bowl, and then wait a few seconds before allowing him to eat with the verbal cue "eat" while pointing at the bowl.

Sit!

Stay!

Eat!

7 **While he is eating, come closer** to the food bowl and pour in a little more dog food or an appetizing treat. He will learn to appreciate your presence near his bowl.

8 **Wait until he is done** eating to remove the food bowl and wash it. Never remove the bowl while your dog is eating, because it will only encourage him to guard his food.

I'm not finished!

Self-Control

All puppies are naturally exuberant, especially when they want to attract attention, play, welcome a friend, cuddle, eat a treat, sniff an interesting scent, and so on. To prevent your puppy from developing bad manners (jumping up on people, barking, pulling on the leash), he must learn canine etiquette, such as how to sit down and act calm before getting what he wants, such as a treat, a toy, petting, or playtime.

TEACH HIM TO CALMLY GREET VISITORS

For this training, the dog must know the Sit and Stay cues, and the visitor must be willing to participate in the lesson. For your dog to learn and retain the lesson, you must repeat and practice it.

1 When the doorbell rings, the puppy will rush to the door.

DING DONG

2 Cue him to sit next to you and, once he is sitting, reward him with "good" and a treat and then give him the Stay cue.

Sit!

Good!

Stay!

3 Open the door.

THE VET'S ADVICE

Be careful: even a very well-trained dog, if highly motivated by something (e.g., the urge to find a female dog in heat or chase a cat) may act on his impulses rather than sitting and waiting for permission.

4 While the dog is still sitting, say "good" and ask the visitor to give the dog a treat.

3 Once the leash is relaxed, take a treat out of your pocket and say "heel."

Heel!

Good!

4 When he is in Heel position, say "good!"

TEACH HIM TO WAIT FOR WHAT HE WANTS

For this training, the dog must know the Heel cue (see page 136). He is learning that he cannot get everything he wants right away, especially when he is on leash and there is a delay between expressing and responding to his needs.

1 The dog pulls on the leash because he detected an interesting scent on a lamppost.

I want to sniff that nice scent!

5 Walk toward the lamppost to let your dog sniff it (reward).

2 Stay still, do not say anything, and do not look at your dog, but wait for him to stop pulling (see Negative Punishment, page 78).

🐾➕ THE VET'S ADVICE

Dogs that cope well with frustration are better able to satisfy their needs, especially in terms of recreational activities.

The Collar, Muzzle, and Harness

EASY
1

MEDIUM
2

MEDIUM
3

His collar is one of the first things a puppy needs to become familiar with, and it is sometimes useful (or required) for him to wear a muzzle as well.

THE COLLAR

Teach your puppy to wear a collar as soon as you bring him home. The collar is one of the first gifts you will give him. He will outgrow his puppy collar, so don't get anything too fancy just yet.

1 Choose a light, comfortable collar. Place it around your puppy's neck and adjust it, ensuring that you can slide two fingers between the collar and his neck.

2 **Distract the puppy** with his favorite toy as you leave the collar on for a few minutes. Gradually increase the duration that he wears the collar until he is used to it.

2, 4, 8, 12... MINUTES

THE MUZZLE

You may find yourself in situations in which it is convenient to muzzle your dog; in other situations, it may be necessary.

Make sure that the muzzle is well-suited to his head shape and is very comfortable. For the dog to accept it willingly, it must be combined with a reward.

1 Place a treat inside.

2 Ask the dog to get the treat.

Take the treat!

3 When he gets used to putting his nose in the muzzle, put his leash on and let him wear the muzzle for a few minutes. Gradually increase the duration.

THE HARNESS

For small dogs with fragile necks and dogs with heart or respiratory conditions, a harness is preferable to a collar because it does not put any pressure on the neck and trachea.

1 Adjust the body strap first and then the neck and chest straps.

2 Make sure you can pass two or three fingers under the neck and body straps. The body strap should be located behind the shoulders but not behind the rib cage.

3 To get your dog used to wearing a harness, do the same training as for the collar.

Walking on Leash

In most regions, laws require dogs to be kept on leash in public places. To avoid being pulled along by your dog and to ensure that walks with him are pleasurable for both of you, start training him to walk politely on leash as soon as he is used to wearing his collar.

KEEP THE LEASH LOOSE

Choose a sturdy, lightweight leash about 4 to 6 feet (1.2 to 1.8 m) long that is comfortable for you to hold.

TEACH THE HEEL CUE

1 **Hold a treat** in your left hand, next to your leg. Call your puppy and lure him with the treat to position himself near your left leg.

2 **When he is in the correct position,** say " good" and give him the treat. Once he understands what you want him to do, start using the verbal cue "heel" and a hand signal (a small tap on the side of your leg, for example) and give him a treat when he comes to Heel position.

   At the beginning of training, when your dog stands at your side, help him learn what you expect from him by consistently rewarding him with "good" followed

Good!

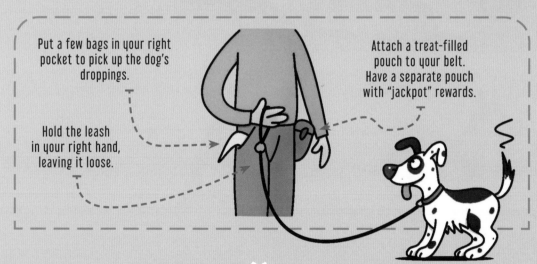

Put a few bags in your right pocket to pick up the dog's droppings.

Hold the leash in your right hand, leaving it loose.

Attach a treat-filled pouch to your belt. Have a separate pouch with "jackpot" rewards.

by a treat. Once he understands the Heel cue, keep rewarding him with praise every time but gradually reduce the frequency of the treats (see Positive Reinforcement [Reward], page 64).

(see Positive Reinforcement [Reward], page 64)

LET'S DO IT!

1 **Start walking slowly,** with the dog on leash on your left side. Show him a treat. He will follow you.

Heel!

Good!

2 Say "heel" and, as soon as he is in **Heel position,** praise him with "good" and give him a treat.

3 **Step forward and, if he stays at your side, reward him with praise and a treat at every step** until he understands what you expect from him.

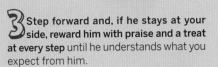

Good!

Come on, Bobby!

4 **Talk to him** to focus his attention on you and avoid distractions. Gradually start to space out the rewards.

5 Once your dog is walking reliably at Heel, **change your pace and start incorporating corners into your walk.**

MAINTAIN HIS MOTIVATION WITH JACKPOTS

To keep your dog focused on you and to avoid frustrating him, start his leash training in a quiet place with few distractions (such as in your yard or around your neighborhood at a quiet time of day), and then gradually increase the difficulty.

Resisting bigger distractions makes the dog even more appreciative of the rewards. Always carry jackpot rewards to keep him motivated (see The Jackpot, page 68); only an extra-special treat can overcome his desire to chase a cat.

(see The Jackpot, page 68)

GET HIM USED TO THE SOUNDS OF THE STREET

If your puppy comes from a farm in the country and is not used to city noises, start by taking him out for walks on Sunday mornings, when there is less traffic and fewer crowds, and then gradually increase the distractions you expose him to **until you are able to walk him on busy Friday nights with no problems.**

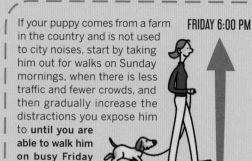

FRIDAY 6:00 PM

SUNDAY 8:00 A.M.

STIMULATION INTENSITY

HOW DO I REACT IF THE DOG PULLS?

If you allow your dog to pull you around and go wherever he wants to go, he will consider it a good strategy and continue to pull, and this **behavior will be reinforced.** To prevent this from happening, two training techniques are recommended.

I can just pull to go anywhere I want!

TECHNIQUE #1: BE A STATUE

1 **Stop,** stand still like a statue, and look away until your dog stops pulling. This is negative punishment because its purpose is to reduce the frequency of the bad behavior—in this case, pulling on the leash—by taking away something pleasant (the walk) from the dog.

2 **When your dog turns** toward you and releases the pressure on the leash, take a treat out of your pocket, hold it at your left side, and say "heel."

Heel!

Darn it! The walk is over.

Good!

3 **When your dog is in Heel position at your side,** say "good," give him the treat, and then start walking again.

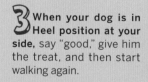

Great! Treats!

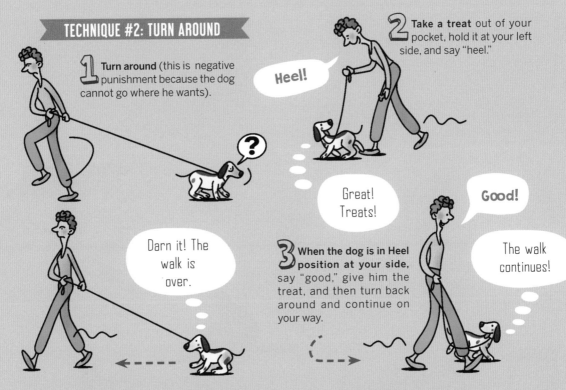

TECHNIQUE #2: TURN AROUND

1 Turn around (this is negative punishment because the dog cannot go where he wants).

2 Take a treat out of your pocket, hold it at your left side, and say "heel."

Heel!

Great! Treats!

Good!

The walk continues!

Darn it! The walk is over.

3 When the dog is in Heel position at your side, say "good," give him the treat, and then turn back around and continue on your way.

TEACH HIM TO STAY CALM WHEN HE SEES THE LEASH

Chances are that the leash will quickly become a powerful signal for your puppy to announce one of his favorite activities. Overwhelmed by his emotions, he may find it difficult to control himself and may become overly excited in every sense of the word. It is important to teach your puppy to exercise self-control when you get his leash, even if only to allow you to easily attach the leash to his collar.

Reinforce good behavior

2 Remain still like a statue and wait until he calms down (see Extinction, page 188). Once he is calm, cue him to sit (do not forget that canine etiquette requires him to sit before getting something he wants).

Sit!

3 When he is sitting, get the leash (this rewards him for his polite behavior), attach it to his collar, and go for a walk.

Great! We're going to go for a walk!

Discourage bad behavior

1 Get the leash. If your dog barks or starts jumping around, ignore him and put the leash away. This is a negative punishment (the dog is deprived of the walk).

Oh no! We're not going for a walk.

Nail Clipping and Other Grooming

Whether you are teaching your dog to let you clip his nails, brush his coat, or perform any other grooming task, the principle is always the same: to gradually get your dog used to the equipment and handling, proceeding in stages, and rewarding him at each stage. Start this training as early as possible with your puppy.

GET HIM USED TO GROOMING EQUIPMENT

Show your puppy the brush, nail clippers, or tooth-brush before feeding him. This will allow him to associate the equipment with the promise of a good meal. Repeat several times.

CLIPPING HIS NAILS IN STAGES

1 Put the nail clipper near the dog.

2 Reward him. Repeat several times.

3 Touch and slightly pinch one nail with the nail clipper, gradually increasing the pressure, and then reward your puppy. Repeat several times.

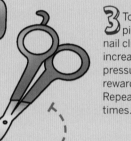

4 Cut one nail and then reward the dog. Repeat with each nail until you can clip all of them.

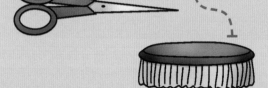

Be patient and take the grooming session slowly. Do you not force the process or get angry with your dog.

Visiting the Veterinarian

Your dog will visit the veterinarian regularly throughout his life, especially in puppyhood when he gets his initial series of vaccinations. It is therefore important that your dog and your vet become good friends.

1 **Go to the veterinarian's office** with your dog at times other than when he has an appointment and ask the staff to greet him with kind words and treats. This will prevent your dog from associating visiting the vet with an unpleasant experience.

2 **Take your dog's favorite treats with you** to motivate him to walk through the door and reward him for his good behavior. To increase his motivation for food rewards, limit his food intake before the appointment.

? HOW DOES FEAR OF THE VET EMERGE?

The dog's apprehension is based on a process of classical conditioning: learning as a result of involuntarily pairing a neutral environmental stimulus, such as a white coat, with an unconditioned stimulus, such as a painful injection. Consequently, this triggers an unconditioned response, meaning one that does not require learning (salivation, increased heart rate, sweating, chills, vomiting, bowel movements) and/or emotion (fear, excitement, happiness).

After several unpleasant veterinary visits, the dog associates the white coat with injections and painful handling. The sight of the vet's white coat then triggers a conditioned reaction of fear. The dog refuses to enter the exam room, he starts shaking and panting, and his heart rate accelerates. In short, he learns to be afraid of the vet. He may even want to walk on the other side of the street when passing by the veterinary clinic.

3 **If your puppy is particularly anxious,** you can, before the appointment, put a calming pheromone-infused collar on him, give him a stress-relieving nutritional supplement, or dress him in a snug-fitting anti-anxiety wrap or vest that exerts a soothing pressure around his chest.

4 **If you are more nervous about the vet than your dog is,** confide in someone to help you get over your anxiety; otherwise, your dog may become overwhelmed by your stress when he is on the examination table.

5 **During your puppy's first visit for an exam or vaccinations,** the staff and vet should be welcoming, offer treats and petting, and take special care with any handling that could be uncomfortable for the dog. Discuss sedatives or anesthesia for unavoidably painful procedures.

Riding in the Car

Your dog's first car ride can sometimes result in nausea and vomiting. After one or more uncomfortable trips, on the basis of classical conditioning, the dog will associate the car with feeling sick and may start vomiting before the car starts or even refuse to get in, knowing what to expect.

1 Get your puppy used to the car from an early age (ideally, your breeder will have already started the process before the pup comes home with you).

2 Make sure that he associates the car with **pleasurable experiences**. Use the car to bring him to the park instead of to the vet's office.

3 Entice him into the stationary car with treats and then play with him, pet him, and give him more treats.

4 Make your dog feel comfortable by distracting him with petting and treats during the ride.

5 Drive calmly. Take short breaks to get out of the car and play.

6 Do not punish him if he vomits or whines during the trip.

7 To prevent him from feeling motion sickness, give him an anti-nausea medication prescribed by the veterinarian.

8 To reassure your dog, bring along one of his canine friends who likes the car.

POSITIVE EXPERIENCES

Dogs do not always associate cars with unpleasant experiences. Think of the dog who hears the sound of the car pulling into the driveway and runs to the door, wagging his tail, because he has associated this noise with the pleasure of his owner returning home. Think of the hunting dog who climbs happily into the car to spend the day doing his job with his owner.

Giving Up a Toy

MEDIUM

1 **Your dog holds his ball in his mouth.** Present him with a treat he loves. He will be more motivated to eat the treat than to keep the ball.

2 **As soon as he drops the ball,** say "give it," praise him, and throw the treat away from the ball.

The purpose of this training is to make your dog understand that if he gives up his toy, he will get a reward and will also get his toy back.

3 **Pick up the ball** and, once he has eaten the treat, show him the ball and then throw it for him to fetch.

4 **Repeat the process several times** until he understands the cue "give it." Once he is responding correctly, combine the verbal cue with a hand signal (holding out your open hand or pointing at the ground).

WIN–WIN SITUATION

Secondary reward

Primary reward

Interrupting Behavior

Stop!

You must issue the verbal cue "stop" firmly but calmly, without anger, and in a nonthreatening way. This is not a punishment.

STEP 1: ASSOCIATE "STOP" WITH A REWARD

While next to your dog, say "stop" and immediately give him a treat. Repeat this several times a day for several days.

This cue is useful on a daily basis; it allows you to interrupt all kinds of behavior and redirect your dog to what you want him to do.

Stop!

Good!

STEP 2: ADD DISTANCE AND DISTRACTION

1 While your dog is busy a few feet (about a meter) away from you—for example, sniffing something in the yard—say "stop" and show him a treat.

2 When he comes to you, say "good" and give him the treat. Repeat the process several times a day for several days.

Make sure that your dog does not become so occupied with an activity that it puts him in danger.

Good!

STEP 3: INCREASE THE LEVEL OF DIFFICULTY

Start to interrupt your dog during increasingly demanding activities. Throw him a toy. Before he gets it, say "stop" and show him a treat. When he comes to you, say "good" and give him the treat.

The more engaging the interrupted activity, the greater the reward should be.

Stop!

Look at Me

The Look at Me cue is very useful in everyday life. It captures your dog's attention when, for example, you want to give him a cue or initiate a game. The training technique used for Look at Me is behavior capturing.

1 Stand in front of your dog and watch him.

2 When he looks at you, praise him by saying "good" and give him a treat. Once he is looking at you repeatedly, introduce the verbal cue "look at me" (see Behavior Capturing, page 127). To help him look at you, guide his gaze toward your face by having him follow your index finger. To avoid making him feel uncomfortable, do not require him to look directly into your eyes but simply to look at your face.

Look at me!

Good!

As with all training, the reward is consistent at first but then becomes random after your dog has learned the behvavior.

Advanced Cues and Tricks

From Six Months to One Year 148

A Puppy's Daily Activities 150

Speak and Quiet 151

Leave it 152

Fetch 154

Closing a Door with His Nose 156

Sit Pretty 157

Play Dead 158

High Five 159

A Good Trainer's Secrets 160

breeds, between seven and ten months; and for large breeds, between eleven and fifteen months. Sexual organs develop; pheromone production and body strength increase. The male starts to lift his leg and compete with other male dogs; fights between males are more frequent. The female has her first heat and starts to attract males.

• **Feeding.** Growth slows down as the puppy approaches adult weight and height. Offer a diet suited to his age and size. Feed two meals a day, one in the morning and one in the evening.

• **Sensory development.** All of his senses are at their peak. Your puppy will be increasingly interested in the scents left by his peers, especially sex pheromones.

• **Autonomy.** The puppy becomes attached to all family members rather than just one person. As this happens, defending his family and territory becomes a priority. Wariness of strangers and the unknown increases. His personality is established.

Your puppy is growing, going through adolescence and puberty, becoming attached to his human family, asserting his personality, and starting to look like an adult.

THE PUPPY'S DEVELOPMENT FROM 6 MONTHS TO 1 YEAR

• **Activity.** Young and full of energy, your puppy just wants to learn. It is time to join an agility class and teach him more complex behaviors. This is a significant period when your puppy's training must be solidified.

• **Dentition.** Normally, all of his permanent teeth have erupted by this time. He will continue to enjoy chewing on all kinds of safe chew toys.

• **Sexual maturity.** Puberty marks the transition to adulthood and varies depending on the dog's adult size. For small breeds, it occurs between five and six months; for medium

THE TRAINING PROGRAM

To perfect your puppy's socialization, continue to take him out to all kinds of places and let him meet different people and animals to prevent him from developing a distrust of strangers and any new fears. Avoid stress that causes persistent fears. Keep encouraging your puppy's attachment to all members of the family: do not let him follow just one person around, and make sure that everyone in the family takes part in caring for him. Be clear and consistent about the house rules and make sure that all of his needs are met, especially his needs to engage his instincts, get plenty of exercise and play, and maintain social relationships. Initiate games and petting frequently. Solidify his training by applying the cues he has already learned and teaching him new, more complex, behaviors.

If your puppy is a quick learner, you may have begun some advanced training already. Regardless of how far you want to take your dog's training, keep practicing and reinforcing the basics.

AND THEN WHAT?

This is when you reap the benefits of your work. If your puppy has gone through puberty without any problems and you have trained him well, you have a wonderful and intelligent companion. But his training is not yet complete. As mentioned, you must continue his socialization (isolation can make him fearful or even antisocial), practice the cues he has learned every day, and teach him new ones. That is all your dog asks for! And it may motivate you to know that a dog who stops learning becomes old, while the one who continues learning stays young. A bit like us!

A Puppy's Daily Activities

A HAPPY DOG IS A DOG WHO IS NOT BORED

The need for scheduled activities varies from dog to dog, depending on age, temperament, and breed. Once a dog is past puberty, he needs an average of four to five hours of daily activity. Small companion breeds will be fine with half this amount, while highly active dogs, like sporting and working breeds, require even more. Think about this before you adopt a dog—insufficient activity is a frequent cause of undesirable behavior.

During the training period, you must devote an average of 30 minutes per day to training.

Taking walks 25%
Socializing with friends 10%
Learning 10%
Chewing 15%
Being useful 10%
Playing/exercise 20%
Drinking, eating, relieving himself 10%

Speak and Quiet

DIFFICULT

Paradoxically, it is important to teach the dog to bark, or "speak," before training him to be quiet. The recommended training technique is behavior capturing.

TEACH HIM TO BE QUIET

1 Now that your dog can bark on cue, ask him to bark and then, with treats in hand, wait for him to be quiet.

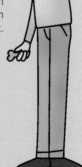

Speak!

Woof!

Woof!

TEACH HIM TO SPEAK

1 Go into a room with your dog and have treats in hand. Pass them back and forth in front of his nose and wait for him to start barking (it should not take long).

Quiet!

2 When he starts barking, say "speak," accompanied by a hand signal (such as holding your hand open), and reward him with praise ("good") and a treat.

2 When he stops barking, put your finger in front of your mouth and say "quiet." Reward him by praising him with "good" and giving him a treat. Repeat several times.

Woof!

Woof!

Good!

Good!

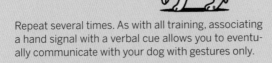

Repeat several times. As with all training, associating a hand signal with a verbal cue allows you to eventually communicate with your dog with gestures only.

As with all training, rewards are initially consistent; once the dog is performing the behavior reliably, the rewards become random.

Leave It

This cue is useful in everyday life because it prevents your dog from eating anything without your permission. It also reinforces the dog's self-control.

STEP 1:
TREAT IN THE HAND

1 Show your closed hand to your dog after hiding an appetizing treat in it.

Something smells good!

2 Your dog will immediately take an interest in your hand and start sniffing it, licking it, or pushing it with his nose. Keep your hand closed.

Leave it.

Good!

3 When your dog loses interest, say "leave it," wait a second, and then praise him with "good."

4 Open your hand, say "take it," and give him the treat. Repeat steps 1–4 several times.

Take it!

5 Gradually increase the interval between the time the dog ignores the treat in your hand and the time you give it to him. As with all training, initially give the reward every time, and then gradually start giving rewards randomly.

1 SECOND, THEN 5, 10, 20, 30...

Please give me that treat!

I'm not a dog who can be easily bought!

6 When the dog is regularly losing interest in the treat in your hand when you give him the Leave It cue, go on to the next phase of training, in which you teach him to ignore a treat placed on the ground.

STEP 2: TREAT ON THE GROUND

1 Drop a treat on the ground.

2 Your dog will rush to eat it.

3 Before he eats it, cover it with your hand. Keep it covered as your dog shows interest.

4 When your dog loses interest, say "leave it," wait a second, and then praise him with "good."

Good!

Leave it!

5 Pick the treat up, open your hand, say "take it," and give him the treat. Repeat several times.

Take it!

Gradually increase the interval between the time the dog ignores the treat on the ground and the time you give it to him.

In learning the Leave It cue, the dog learns that the best way to get what he wants is to ignore it.

Fetch

This training, which is very useful on a daily basis, teaches a complex behavior acquired through shaping. Start by splitting the behavior into several steps, rewarding your dog at each successful step until you get the desired behavior.

1 Start by placing the object (for example, a folded newspaper with a rubber band around it) in a place accessible to your dog (on the edge of the coffee table). Then, observe his behavior.

2 Your dog looks at the object. Praise him with "good" and give him a treat.

Good! ✛ 🦴 Reward

? TRAINING THROUGH BEHAVIOR SHAPING

Shaping is a training method that breaks down a complex behavior into small steps and reinforces the dog at each step as he comes increasingly closer to the desired behavior.

Some complex behaviors, such as fetching an object, closing a door, turning on a light, and putting toys in a basket, involve a series of simple acts that are unlikely to happen naturally, unless your dog is a genius. In these cases, training can be done through shaping.

This method of training is based on the premise that no behavior is too difficult to be broken down into smaller, simple steps. Breaking down the desired behavior into small steps requires a keen sense of observation and a lot of patience. It requires rewarding approximations that approach the desired behavior until the dog achieves it. It forces the dog to think and take initiative.

The closer the dog gets to the target behavior, the greater the reward, while you fade out the rewards for earlier approximations. In the last step, you combine the desired behavior with a verbal cue.

3 Your dog moves toward the object. Praise him with "good" and give him a treat.

Good! ✛ Reward

4 Your dog touches the object with his nose. Praise him with "good" and give him a treat.

Good! ✛ Reward

5 He takes the object in his mouth. Praise him with "good" and give him a treat.

Good! ✛ Reward

6 Your dog brings the object to you. Say "fetch." Praise him with "good" and give him a treat.

Fetch!

Good! ✛ Reward

 GOOD TO KNOW

Rather than simply waiting for your dog to take steps toward the desired behavior on his own, you can help him by using the luring technique (see page 128).

The clicker is ideal for this training because it allows you to indicate each successful step with more precision than other training methods (see Clicker Training, page 69).

7 A quick learner might skip some of these steps, but remember that the closer your dog gets to the objective, the greater the reward. Once he completes a step, you no longer reward the previous step, and so on, until he achieves the final desired behavior.

In the last step of Fetch, you combine the behavior with the verbal cue "fetch" and exchange the object for a treat (see Giving Up a Toy, page 143).

Closing a Door with His Nose

DIFFICULT

The clicker, because of its precision, is particularly well suited to shaping behavior. As with the previous exercise (Fetch), you will break down this behavior into multiple steps, clicking and rewarding for each successful step until you get the desired final behavior. For this exercise, we will use the refrigerator door.

SPLITTING THE BEHAVIOR INTO STEPS

1 The dog looks at the refrigerator. Click and give him a treat.

2 He moves to the refrigerator. Click and give him a treat.

3 He touches the refrigerator door with his nose. Click and give him a treat.

4 He lightly pushes the refrigerator door with his nose. Click and give him a treat.

5 He closes the refrigerator door by pushing it with his nose. Say "close," click, and give him a treat. A quick learner might skip some of these steps on his way to the final behavior.

Close!

The closer the dog is to achieving the objective, the greater the reward. Once he completes a step, you no longer reward the previous step, and so on, until he achieves the final desired behavior.

Sit Pretty

For this lesson, the dog must know the Sit cue. You will use luring for this exercise.

1 Have the dog sit in front of you. Show him a treat and pass it from in front of his nose up to his eye level.

2 **Move the treat upward** until he lifts his front legs up and sits back on his haunches. At this precise moment, praise him with "good" and give him the treat.

Good! + Reward

3 Repeat the exercise, each time waiting for your dog to raise his front legs a little higher and stay in position a little longer before rewarding him.

4 When the dog is consistently performing the desired behavior, introduce the verbal cue "sit pretty" and a hand signal (both hands together, for example) before he does it.

Sit pretty!

As with all training, the rewards are initially consistent; once the dog is performing the behavior reliably, the rewards become random.

Play Dead

For this exercise, you will use the luring technique, and the dog must already know the Down cue.

Down!

1 Give your dog the verbal cue "down."

2 Squat down, with a treat in your hand, and put it behind your dog's neck to encourage him to lie down on his side and put his head on the ground.

3 Once he is lying on his side with his head on the ground, praise him with "good" and give him the treat.

Good! ✚

Reward

4 When the dog understands the exercise after practicing several times, add the cue "play dead" and mimic a pistol with your hand.

Bang, you're dead!

5 When he lies down on his side on your cue, praise him with "good" and give him a treat.

Good!

As with all training, the rewards are initially consistent; once the dog is performing the behavior reliably, the rewards become random.

6 Repeat the exercise several times, increasing the duration of how long the dog lies down before you praise him and give him the treat.

High Five

For this exercise, use shaping to break down the behavior into smaller steps. Reward your dog at each successful step until you achieve the desired behavior.

SPLITTING THE BEHAVIOR INTO STEPS

1 Hide a treat in your hand and encourage your dog to put his paw on your hand.

2 The dog puts his paw on your closed hand on the floor. Praise him with "good" and give him the treat.

Good! + Reward

3 Lift your closed hand up a little. The dog raises his paw halfway and puts it on your closed hand. Praise him with "good" and give him the treat.

Good! + Reward

4 Lift your closed hand up a little more. The dog raises his paw and puts it on your closed hand. Praise him with "good" and give him the treat.

Good! + Reward

GOOD TO KNOW

Another option is to use the clicker for training High Five because it allows you to indicate the behavior you want with more precision than just giving praise and treats (see Clicker Training, page 69).

5 Next, the dog raises his paw and puts it on your open hand. Praise him with "good" and give him a treat.

Good! + Reward

6 Finally, the dog raises his paw and places it flat on your open hand. Say "high five," praise him with "good," and give him a treat.

High five!

Good! + Reward.

If your dog is a quick learner, you may not need to do as many steps. The last step is the final behavior combined with the verbal cue "high five."

A Good Trainer's Secrets

Loving your dog is a prerequisite to being a good trainer, but it is not enough. In addition, you must understand, guide, and respect your dog in accordance with the seven rules implemented by good teachers to motivate their students and help them progress throughout their lives.

Of all a dog owner's responsibilities, the most rewarding is properly training his or her dog.

GOOD TRAINERS HAVE THE ESSENTIAL QUALITIES OF TEACHERS

THEY UNDERSTAND,

They see the world from the dog's point of view to understand the dog's emotions and behavior and act accordingly.

THEY LOVE,

They play, hug, reward, encourage, value, and fulfill the dog's needs to prove their love and strengthen the relationship.

THEY GUIDE.

They define fair rules, clearly state their expectations, and guide the dog with training to help him live in harmony with his surroundings.

GOOD TRAINER

THE SEVEN RULES OF A GOOD TRAINER

1 A good trainer dedicates time to the dog on a daily basis and actively participates in the dog's age-appropriate education.

2 A good trainer loves his or her "student" and builds a relationship of mutual affection and trust.

4 A good trainer rewards the dog for his progress. He or she always has a wide variety of rewards to keep the dog motivated and uses special rewards for great behaviors.

5 A good trainer is always in a good mood when starting a training session. He or she creates a calm atmosphere by limiting the number of distractions, always ends lessons on a positive note, and offers breaks between training sessions.

6 A good trainer forgives mistakes and does not punish bad behavior but instead interrupts it and redirects the dog toward good behavior (see Positive Behavior Modification, page 163).

7 A good trainer teaches new cues and tricks throughout the dog's life and perfects his or her own training techniques day after day.

3 A good trainer is not too demanding and teaches one cue at a time working from the simplest to the most difficult. He or she does short (five-minute) and frequent lessons and repeats the exercises.

Part 5

Positive Behavior Modification

Positive training is not a magical solution. Your dog's behavior depends on not only the training you provide but also other factors that are difficult to control, such as heredity, his living environment, and his health.

If, despite your positive training, your dog displays undesirable behavior, do not interpret it as a display of opposition toward you. Rather, involve the whole family, maintain your relationship of trust with your pet, and analyze the situation. This will help you develop a positive plan of action so that your dog can be a well-behaved member both of his family and of society.

POSITIVE BEHAVIOR MODIFICATION

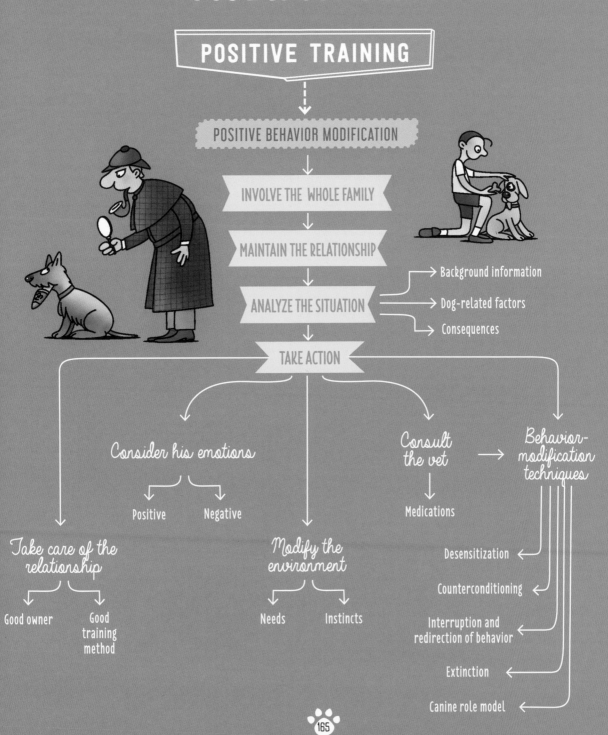

POSITIVE TRAINING

POSITIVE BEHAVIOR MODIFICATION

INVOLVE THE WHOLE FAMILY

MAINTAIN THE RELATIONSHIP

ANALYZE THE SITUATION
→ Background information
→ Dog-related factors
→ Consequences

TAKE ACTION

Consider his emotions
- Positive
- Negative

Consult the vet
- Medications

Behavior-modification techniques

Take care of the relationship
- Good owner
- Good training method

Modify the environment
- Needs
- Instincts

- Desensitization
- Counterconditioning
- Interruption and redirection of behavior
- Extinction
- Canine role model

Maintain the Relationship

Having a dog who displays unpleasant behavior is difficult to accept. Often, due to stress and frustration, our first reflex is to punish, without thinking, when unwanted behavior occurs. It's an easy solution that may be effective in the short term but is certainly ineffective in the long term.

INVOLVE THE WHOLE FAMILY

All family members interact with each other and the dog. Therefore, the dog's undesirable behavior is partly related to and dependent on the behaviors of his family members. For example, if your children give the dog food from the table during family meals, how can you expect him to stay quietly in his bed during dinner? All family members must be involved in the behavior's resolution.

DO NOT PUNISH

By punishing, under the false pretext of maintaining your authority as a leader (see What Makes a Good Owner?, page 23), you worsen your relationship with the dog and exacerbate the problem. The punishment you choose as a solution to the behavior problem then becomes the source of the problem.

Before you get angry, think about the disastrous effects of your attitude on your relationship with your dog. Punishment negatively affects the dog's emotional state and perception of the environment, reduces his ability to learn, causes your relationship to deteriorate, and aggravates the situation (see pages 72–81).

Continually punishing your dog causes him to feel threatened and defensive. This, in turn, will cause you to take additional punitive measures that he will perceive as further evidence of threat, and so on, until he finally retaliates by biting.

Analyze the Situation

The solution to a problem depends on how you look at it. The best way to find out how to effectively modify unwanted behavior is to analyze the elements that cause it to appear and persist, as if you were dismantling a machine to understand how it works. The goal is to discover what is causing the problem to persist so you can adopt an approach that is conducive to change.

INVESTIGATE THOROUGHLY

1 What factors trigger the onset of the undesirable behavior?

Boredom, unfulfilled needs, poor communication, and excessive punishment are common causes of bad behavior. The environment can also contribute to unwanted behavior; examples of this include a dog

2 What are the dog-related factors?

Undesirable behavior can be caused by poor health (physical or psychological illness) or a particular perception of the world that is shaped by the learning process, the training methods used, and the dog's memories, experiences, and living conditions.

3 What are the consequences of the undesirable behavior?

By modifying what happens after the undesirable behavior, you influence the probability of its reappearance. If the consequence is positive for the dog, the behavior will be reinforced; if the consequence is negative, the frequency of the behavior will decrease (see Reward versus Punishment, page 81).

For example, opening the door when the dog barks is like giving him a reward, so do not be surprised if he continues to bark. If the dog is afraid of the mailman, and the mailman goes away every time the dog barks, this is a reward that will encourage the dog to keep barking at the mailman.

I'm bored, so I'm eating your slippers!

Why does he always hang out in front of my house?

If the dog runs away to chase a neighborhood cat, and there is nothing to stop him from doing so, he will persist in trying to get out to chase the cat.

who is abused by ill-mannered children and defends himself by growling in their direction, a dog who runs away from home in pursuit of a female dog in heat, or a puppy raised in the country who refuses to go outside in the city because he is not used to the sounds.

> It takes little intelligence to detect a bad solution, but it takes a lot of intelligence to ask the right questions.

Take Action

In the case of behavioral problems, the leader (you) acts positively to bring about change. You define the problem precisely, identify the elements that led to its emergence and persistence, and then implement positive solutions, taking care to avoid punishment (which you may already have tried without success). In any case, you must set a realistic goal with which you can achieve success (it's pointless to wish that your dog would never bark, for example).

CONSULT YOUR VETERINARIAN

Start by making sure your dog does not have an illness—osteoarthritis, brain tumor, diabetes, hypothyroidism, depression, anxiety, hyperactivity, and so on—that could be the cause of his undesirable behavior. (See When Should Medications Be Used?, page 194). Here are some examples of undesirable behaviors that may have a medical cause.

SITUATION: The dog drinks a lot and urinates a lot in the house.

ACTION: Have a blood test done to look for diabetes or kidney failure.

SITUATION: The dog, previously obedient, no longer responds to basic cues.

ACTION: Test for hearing loss. In this case, you can replace verbal cues with visual signals. (You see here the advantage of always combining a verbal cue with a specific hand gesture).

SITUATION: The dog does damage in the house during your absence.

ACTION: Consult a behavioral specialist to discuss separation anxiety and possible treatments.

MODIFY THE ENVIRONMENT

In some cases, the solution may consist of acting on the event that triggers the annoying behavior but also on the broader context (logistics, schedule changes, better consideration of the dog's needs, and so forth).

SITUATION: The dog digs holes under the fence to join the female dog in heat at your neighbor's house.

ACTION: Ask the neighbors to have their female dog spayed. If the dogs are not spayed/neutered, you will all have to take responsibility for any resulting litters.

SITUATION: The dog scratches at the back door when he is outside and it is raining because he needs shelter.

ACTION: For times when you are not home or cannot let him indoors, make sure that your dog has a comfortable doghouse in the yard.

SITUATION: The dog barks when he sees passersby from behind the fence.

ACTION: Remove your dog's access to parts of the yard where the fenceline runs alongside the sidewalk.

CHANGE YOUR RELATIONSHIP: BE A GOOD OWNER

Be honest about your relationship with your dog. A relationship that is nonexistent or diminished by punishment, poor communication, or a lack of consistency (see Establish Clear and Fair Rules, page 40) will inevitably lead to behavioral problems. A weak relationship between the owner and the dog provides the framework that serves as a starting point (change the relationship) to find a solution (solve the behavioral problem).

As dog owners, we can solve many behavioral problems when we understand that we are partly responsible for these problems. When a dog does not respond to his owner's cues, most of the time it is not the actual cue that he is ignoring (which corresponds to basic communication, i.e., the exchange of information) but the relationship (or lack thereof) established between him and his owner (higher level of communication).

Focus on Positive Leadership

Be a positive leader, love your dog, meet his needs, understand his perspective, and communicate clearly, and you will build a strong relationship and thus avoid many behavioral problems. A close and stable relationship of trust is essential for you and your dog to cohabitate harmoniously. The better the relationship, the smoother and easier the communication.

It has long been believed that the relationship between humans and dogs is built solely on a hierarchy of linear dominance, which leads the owner to position him- or herself as the "pack leader," especially when trying to solve behavioral problems: "I am the leader; you are at my command, and you must obey me." In this model, the dog must submit in any situation and will be punished if he does not obey.

This dominator-dominated relationship is simple to understand, is easy to implement, and does not factor in the dog's emotional state. It also opens the door to all kinds of abuse (punishment, threats, aggression). If the dog gets on the couch, growls, or disobeys, according to this theory, the only solutions would be for the leader to resolve the issue by force or by taking the dog's resources away from him. But this type of relationship causes a dog to distrust his owner and plunges the dog into a state of insecurity. It causes anxiety and promotes aggression rather than preventing it! A relationship based on positive leadership, on the contrary, boosts the dog's sense of security, gives him confidence in his owner, and motivates him to do well.

> The desire to punish is indicative of a feeling of helplessness when faced with a situation. Understanding the situation makes this feeling and the accompanying desire to punish disappear.

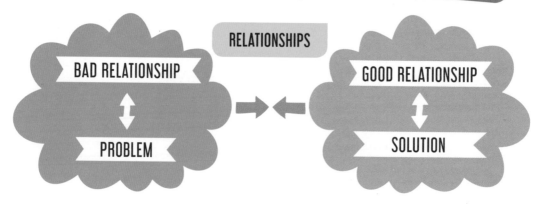

RELATIONSHIPS

BAD RELATIONSHIP ↕ PROBLEM → ← GOOD RELATIONSHIP ↕ SOLUTION

Consider Your Dog's Instincts and Emotions

In all cases, the solution to a behavioral problem requires considering the dog's instinctive needs and acknowledging the dog's feelings in difficult situations.

INSTINCT-RELATED BEHAVIORS

Certain motor behaviors (chasing, fetching, pointing, capturing, chewing, nibbling, biting, smelling) can be linked to instinctive patterns existing at birth (see Understand His Instincts, page 48). They facilitate the emergence of physical behaviors that are specific to the dog. These behaviors have often been augmented by humans to obtain breeds with particular aptitudes (hunting, guarding, retrieving, tracking).

The dog's motivation to perform these behaviors has been genetically programmed. Their expression depends on the physical characteristics of the dog (height, weight, muscle tone), the dog's experiences, and the demands of the dog's environment but can never be totally suppressed. If the dog is unable to perform his instinctive duties, he needs to be provided with similar alternatives.

The Desire to Chew

Of course, all dogs, whether you like it or not, have a somewhat strong propensity to chew anything they can put in their mouths. If no suitable chew toys are available to a dog, the dog will satisfy his urge to chew by sinking his teeth into table legs, your shoes, or any other object within his reach.

Failure to fulfill your dog's instinctive needs is a frequent source of unwanted behavior.

UNFULFILLED INSTINCTS ➡ NEEDS ➡ UNDESIRABLE BEHAVIOR

SITUATION: The dog chews on the legs of a table.

ACTION: When you cannot supervise, keep the dog in a puppy-proofed room with plenty of safe chew toys. Use a chew-deterrent product on the table legs to make them less appealing. Always have suitable chew toys and treat-filled toys available to the dog.

> Modifying undesirable behavior means understanding the need driving the behavior.

YOUR DOG'S EMOTIONS

Emotions determine an individual's reaction to events. The dog's emotional brain reacts instantly and triggers immediate reactions in his body.

When emotions overwhelm your dog, he can be trapped in his emotional brain, without control over his emotions; punishing him without dealing with his emotional state will only lead to misunderstanding, a deterioration of the relationship, and what could be a dangerous escalation of events. Punishing a dog without changing his emotions is like trying to stop a speeding car by shooting the tires. You will slow it down, but you will not stop it from crashing.

For your dog to regain control of his emotions, you must divert his attention toward something else or remove him from the triggering factor by changing his environment (see Modify the Environment, page 169).

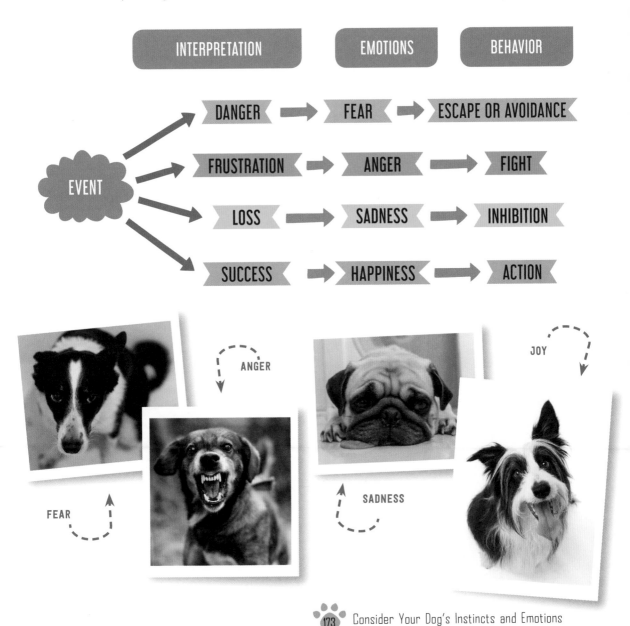

| INTERPRETATION | EMOTIONS | BEHAVIOR |

EVENT

DANGER → FEAR → ESCAPE OR AVOIDANCE

FRUSTRATION → ANGER → FIGHT

LOSS → SADNESS → INHIBITION

SUCCESS → HAPPINESS → ACTION

FEAR

ANGER

SADNESS

JOY

THE DOG REFUSES TO GIVE UP HIS BALL: BAD ATTITUDE

No one touches my ball!

Grrr...

SITUATION: You want to take a ball—or any other toy—from your dog, and he does not want to give it up. He becomes angry and growls.

I am in charge! He must obey!

NEGATIVE EMOTION

You're afraid, so you don't do anything.

I've made myself clear. My strategy is best.

You don't try to understand the reason for his anger, and you punish him and take his ball by force.

The next time the situation arises, the dog will behave in the same way.

PUNISHMENT

He didn't understand me. This is my favorite ball, and now I'm sad.

Grrr...

NEGATIVE EMOTION

The next time the situation arises, the dog will behave differently.

Grrr...

NEGATIVE EMOTION

More aggression. This behavior leads to an escalation of violence.

NEGATIVE EMOTION

Inhibition and its corollaries: stress and anxiety. This behavior wrongly reinforces the master's punitive attitude.

THE DOG REFUSES TO GIVE UP HIS BALL: GOOD ATTITUDE

SITUATION: You want to take a ball—or any other toy—from your dog, and he does not want to give it up. He becomes angry and growls.

You understand his anger and his motivation to keep his beloved toy. To make him drop the ball, you show him his favorite treat.

The dog is more motivated to taste the treat than to keep the ball. As he drops the ball, praise him and throw the treat away from the ball. Take the ball. Once he has eaten the treat, show him the ball and then throw it for him to fetch.

It is a win-win situation.

Grrr...

NEGATIVE EMOTION

Your actions cause an emotional change

Good!

POSITIVE EMOTION

YOUR DOG DOESN'T WANT TO GO NEAR A BIGGER DOG: GOOD ATTITUDE

SITUATION: While approaching another dog and owner while on a walk, your dog shows signs of anxiety (hypervigilance, lip licking, slow gait).

You understand that your dog is disturbed by the sight of another dog. You then decide either to move away from the other dog (change his environment) so he regains his calm, or to capture the dog's attention with something pleasant, such as a treat or a toy, to reduce his apprehension (change his emotion).

Change of environment

Come on! If you're not comfortable, we're leaving.

His owner seems cool!

Change of emotion

USE BEHAVIOR MODIFICATION TECHNIQUES

You can't stop your dog from feeling emotions in certain circumstances; however, you can change his emotions and his behavior through behavior modification techniques. These techniques, which we will discuss in the following section, help change the dog's perspective of his environment. They allow the dog to form new and positive associations with situations that he previously viewed negatively so that he no longer feels the need to behave in an undesirable way. New learning replaces the old, and new synaptic connections are created.

SITUATION: The dog is afraid of children and growls at the sight of them.

ACTION: Transform his negative association with children into a positive one by using desensitization combined with counterconditioning.

Regardless of the intensity level of the behavior modification techniques, they change the way the dog interprets information from his environment at the cerebral level, and thus change his behavior.

TRY DIFFERENT LEVELS OF ACTION TO CHANGE UNDESIRABLE BEHAVIOR

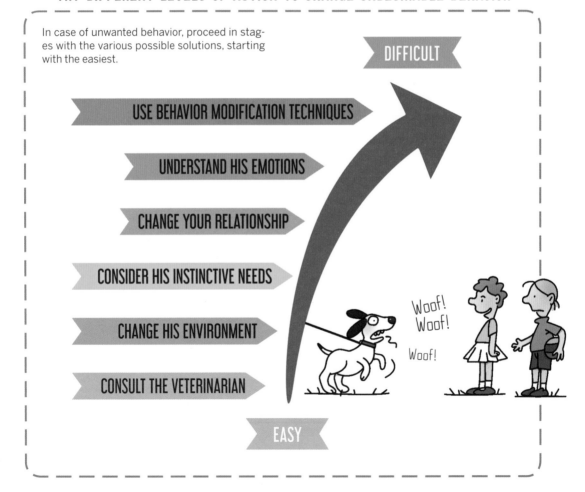

In case of unwanted behavior, proceed in stages with the various possible solutions, starting with the easiest.

DIFFICULT

USE BEHAVIOR MODIFICATION TECHNIQUES

UNDERSTAND HIS EMOTIONS

CHANGE YOUR RELATIONSHIP

CONSIDER HIS INSTINCTIVE NEEDS

CHANGE HIS ENVIRONMENT

CONSULT THE VETERINARIAN

EASY

Woof! Woof! Woof!

Behavior Modification Techniques

Desensitization 180

Counterconditioning 183

Interruption and Redirection 187

Extinction 188

A Canine Role Model 190

How Long Does Behavioral Change Take? 191

Summary of Techniques... 192

When Should Medications Be Used?.................................. 194

Desensitization

Desensitization is used to treat fears and phobias (of cars, storms, children, other dogs, vacuum cleaners, umbrellas, and so on). It is based on training by habituation, meaning that you will get the dog used to the object of his fears gradually, in stages.

WHAT IS IT ABOUT?

This method consists of exposing the dog repeatedly and gradually to the object of his fear (trigger), in short sessions, so that he remains calm and relaxed (in a comfort zone, or green zone) without displaying an arousal reaction (in a blue zone, or comfort limit) or fear, escape, or aggression (in a red zone, or uncomfortable zone). The goal is for the dog's emotional brain to record that there is no danger. The method is often used with counterconditioning.

GRADUALLY INCREASE THE INTENSITY OF THE TRIGGER

For the first session, be sure to present the fear trigger at a level of intensity that is low enough to not provoke a fear reaction (staying in the dog's comfort zone), and then slightly increase the intensity. Start each new level with a slightly lower intensity than the previous level before gradually increasing the intensity. The maximum intensity you want to achieve corresponds to the trigger's natural intensity in the dog's environment.

ADJUST THE INTENSITY

The more you are able to adjust the intensity of the trigger, the greater the chances of success. Adjust the intensity to correspond with exposure time and include the five senses: sight, hearing, touch, smell, and taste.

ADJUST THE DISTANCE

Gradually reduce the distance between your dog and the trigger (child, other dog, vacuum cleaner).

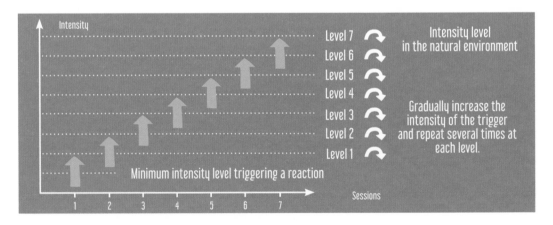

Intensity

Level 7 — Intensity level in the natural environment
Level 6
Level 5
Level 4
Level 3 — Gradually increase the intensity of the trigger and repeat several times at each level.
Level 2
Level 1

Minimum intensity level triggering a reaction

Sessions
1 2 3 4 5 6 7

ADJUST THE SIZE

Gradually increase the size of the trigger (umbrella, ball).

ADJUST THE SOUND

Gradually increase the volume of the trigger (hair dryer, vacuum cleaner, recorded storm sounds).

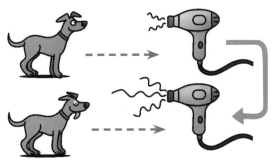

ADJUST THE PRESSURE

Gradually increase the pressure of the trigger (brush, comb, nail clippers, petting).

ADJUST THE DURATION

Gradually increase the duration for which you expose your dog to the trigger.

STAY IN THE DOG'S COMFORT ZONE

If the dog goes into a state of arousal and shows the beginning signs of fear (blue zone), divert his attention and, if necessary, slightly reduce the intensity of the trigger (increase the distance, decrease the volume, reduce the size) to prevent him from being overwhelmed by his fear or anger and allow him to regain his calm. The desensitization session must always end calmly or else his fear will increase.

THE DIFFERENT ZONES

RED ZONE: UNCOMFORTABLE ZONE

ANGER — Much too intense

FEAR — Too intense

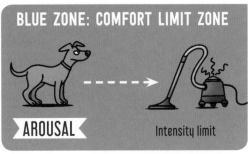

BLUE ZONE: COMFORT LIMIT ZONE

AROUSAL — Intensity limit

If the dog goes into a state of arousal, return to the green zone.

GREEN ZONE: COMFORT ZONE

CALM — Suitable intensity

PRACTICAL APPLICATION: DESENSITIZATION TO CHILDREN

THE DIFFERENT STAGES OF PROGRESSION

At the final stage, the dog should take treats from a child's hand.

7   Allow him to be pet by a child and accept treats from the child's hand

6   Approach a group of children 5 feet (1.5 m) away

5   Approach a group of children 10 feet (3 m) away

4   Approach a group of children 15 feet (4.5 m) away

3   Approach a group of children 20 feet (6 m) away

2   Approach a group of children 25 feet (about 7.5 m) away

1   Approach a group of children 30 feet (9 m) away

LEVEL 1

At a distance from a group of children (comfort zone), approach to about 30 feet (9 m) away and monitor your dog's reactions. You want him to be calm, relaxed, and feeling safe, with his ears in a natural position, tail at rest, and mouth slightly open. He should breathe calmly, with a slow gait, and should look at the children while also taking an interest in the environment. Stay at this distance for fifteen minutes and then slowly move away from the group of children. Repeat this exercise for several days at the same distance before proceeding to Level 2.

 Ideal condition

30 FEET (9 M): COMFORT DISTANCE

GREEN ZONE

LEVEL 2

Start about 30 feet (9 m) from the group of children and progress to 25 feet (7.5 m) away while monitoring your dog's reactions.

The dog stays in the green zone:
Repeat the exercise for several days at a distance of 25 feet (7.5 m) and then move on to Level 3 and beyond.

The dog enters the blue zone:
He is on the alert, with ears upright, tail slightly straightened, eyelids wide open, and eyes fixed on the group of children.

Divert your dog's attention by talking to him. If necessary, move back to 30 feet (9 m) from the group of children so that he can regain his calm (green zone). Repeat the exercise as many days as needed until he stays in the green zone at 25 feet (7.5 m). Then repeat at this distance for several days before moving on the next level, gradually progressing to Level 7.

 Comfort limit reached

25 FEET (7.5 M): COMFORT LIMIT

BLUE ZONE

Counterconditioning

With this method, you help the dog adopt behavior that is emotionally and physiologically incompatible with the behavior to be suppressed. This technique is often used with desensitization.

WHEN TO USE COUNTERCONDITIONING?

This technique is used to treat fears and phobias. It allows the dog to change his emotional response (anger, fear) to certain problematic situations (emotional stimuli) through the formation of new, positive associations with these stimuli.

The situation does not change, but the dog's interpretation of it is modified. In the case of fear treatment, the goal is for the dog to adopt a positive outlook on a formerly anxiety-inducing situation.

THE DOG'S MAIN PHOBIAS

To avoid the development of phobias (irrational fears), early habituation to the environment is essential (see Acclimate Him to His Environment, page 106).

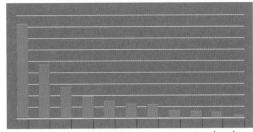

Sudden loud noise · Storm · Vehicle · Human · Bright light · Rain · Telephone · Bike · Veterinarian · Wind · Bird

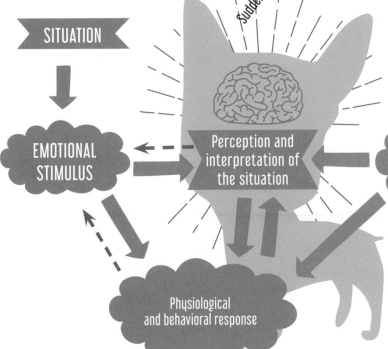

SITUATION

EMOTIONAL STIMULUS

Perception and interpretation of the situation

Counterconditioning + desensitization

Physiological and behavioral response

PRACTICAL APPLICATION:
COUNTERCONDITIONING AND DESENSITIZATION

SITUATION: THE DOG IS AFRAID OF TRUCKS

STARTING POINT: The dog thinks trucks are dangerous.

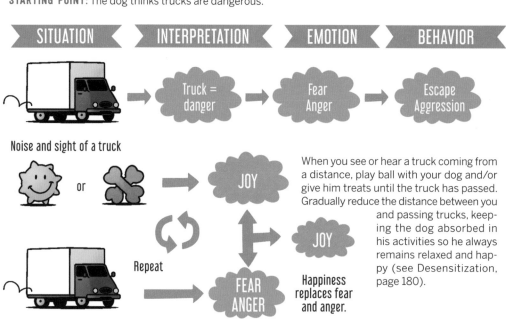

| SITUATION | INTERPRETATION | EMOTION | BEHAVIOR |

Noise and sight of a truck

Repeat

JOY

JOY

FEAR ANGER

Happiness replaces fear and anger.

When you see or hear a truck coming from a distance, play ball with your dog and/or give him treats until the truck has passed. Gradually reduce the distance between you and passing trucks, keeping the dog absorbed in his activities so he always remains relaxed and happy (see Desensitization, page 180).

AFTER COUNTERCONDITIONING COMBINED WITH DESENSITIZATION: The dog thinks that trucks bring him good things.

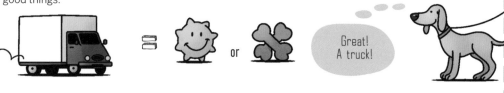

Great! A truck!

| SITUATION | INTERPRETATION | EMOTION | BEHAVIOR |

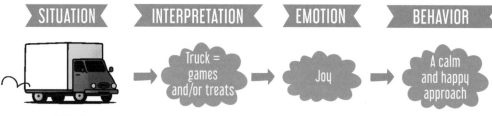

Truck = games and/or treats → Joy → A calm and happy approach

Noise and sight of a truck

SITUATION: THE DOG IS AFRAID OF THE VACUUM CLEANER

STARTING POINT: The dog thinks the vacuum cleaner is a monster.

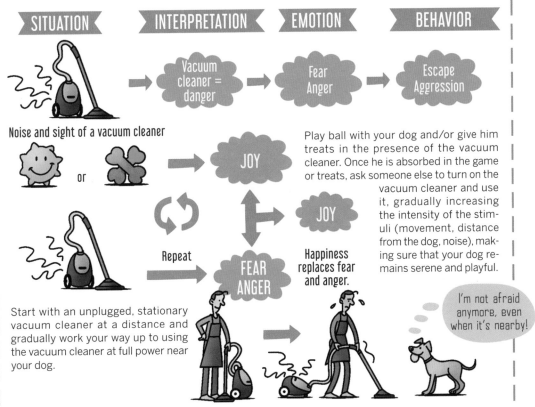

SITUATION → **INTERPRETATION** → **EMOTION** → **BEHAVIOR**

Vacuum cleaner = danger → Fear Anger → Escape Aggression

Noise and sight of a vacuum cleaner

JOY

or → JOY

Repeat → FEAR ANGER → Happiness replaces fear and anger.

Play ball with your dog and/or give him treats in the presence of the vacuum cleaner. Once he is absorbed in the game or treats, ask someone else to turn on the vacuum cleaner and use it, gradually increasing the intensity of the stimuli (movement, distance from the dog, noise), making sure that your dog remains serene and playful.

I'm not afraid anymore, even when it's nearby!

Start with an unplugged, stationary vacuum cleaner at a distance and gradually work your way up to using the vacuum cleaner at full power near your dog.

AFTER COUNTERCONDITIONING COMBINED WITH DESENSITIZATION: The dog thinks that the vacuum cleaner brings him good things.

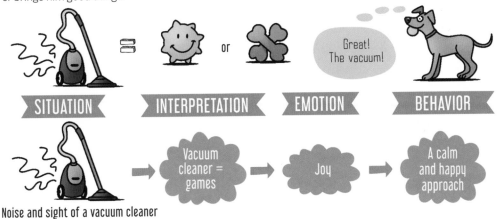

= or

Great! The vacuum!

SITUATION → **INTERPRETATION** → **EMOTION** → **BEHAVIOR**

Noise and sight of a vacuum cleaner

Vacuum cleaner = games → Joy → A calm and happy approach

SITUATION: THE DOG IS AFRAID OF LARGE DOGS

STARTING POINT: The dog thinks that bigger dogs are not his friends.

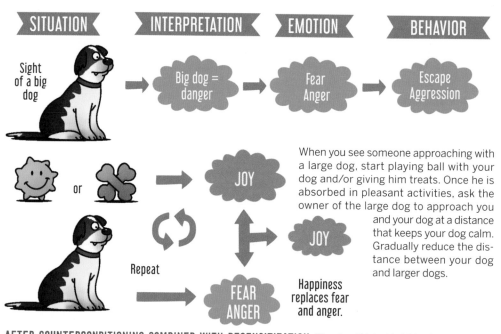

When you see someone approaching with a large dog, start playing ball with your dog and/or giving him treats. Once he is absorbed in pleasant activities, ask the owner of the large dog to approach you and your dog at a distance that keeps your dog calm. Gradually reduce the distance between your dog and larger dogs.

AFTER COUNTERCONDITIONING COMBINED WITH DESENSITIZATION: The dog thinks that big dogs bring him good things.

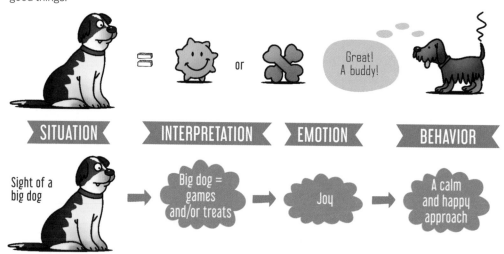

Interruption and Redirection

Interrupting unwanted behavior is useful in everyday life. You can do it by saying "no" in a firm tone, clapping your hands, whistling or making another noise, or distracting the dog with a game or toy.

REDIRECT THE DOG

To reduce the frequency of undesirable behavior, you should use the act of interrupting the behavior to capture the dog's attention and redirect him to desirable behavior for which you can reward him. The dog learns that some behaviors are not acceptable, while others are encouraged. Thus, through repetition, the dog learns and remembers the rules of life.

DON'T ABUSE THE WORD "NO"

To maintain the effectiveness of "no" and other behavior-interruption stimuli, use them appropriately and always pair them with the redirection of the behavior; otherwise, once the surprise of the interruption is over, the dog will return to the unwanted behavior. Behavior interruptors should never be combined with punishment, as this may cause fear and confusion in the dog's mind.

SITUATION: THE DOG BARKS WHEN THE PHONE RINGS

Step 1: Interrupt the behavior.

Step 2: Redirect the behavior to something desirable that you can reward; for example, give him the Sit cue, praise him, and give him a treat.

SITUATION: THE DOG CHEWS ON ELECTRICAL CORDS

Step 1: Interrupt the behavior.

Step 2: Redirect the behavior to something desirable that you can reward; for example, give him something acceptable to chew on and praise him when he chews on it. Usually, if you provide the dog with something to satisfy his natural need to chew, he will not have to look for something in his environment to satisfy this desire. Knowing and fulfilling your dog's natural needs helps prevent many undesirable behaviors.

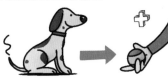

Extinction

Extinction consists of eliminating undesirable behavior by removing its positive consequences (positive reinforcements). It is particularly suitable for eliminating attention-seeking behaviors: barking for you to open the door, nudging you to get food from the table, jumping up to get petting, and the like. To be more effective, extinction must be combined with rewarding an alternative, acceptable behavior so that the dog will still get the positive reinforcement he is seeking.

IDENTIFY ALL REINFORCEMENTS

Food, petting, eye contact, attention, talking to the dog: you must definitively and permanently remove all positive reinforcements (intentional or not) that perpetuate undesirable behavior.

BE FIRM

Initially, it is common to see an increase in the frequency and intensity of the behavior, known as " the extinction peak," but remain stoic! If you give in to your dog, you will be using intermittent reinforcement (see Unintentional Rewards, page 70), which only reinforces the behavior you want to eliminate. Pairing extinction with the reinforcement of a desirable behavior that has the same outcome as the unwanted behavior reduces the extinction peak. For example, you can teach your dog to **sit in front of the back door** instead of barking to get you to open the door.

IGNORE HIM

The best way not to reinforce the dog's behavior is to pay no attention to him. Stay still, without looking at him, until he calms down, or leave the room.

SITUATION: THE DOG JUMPS UP TO GET ATTENTION

STARTING POINT:
The dog thinks that, to get attention, he has to play the clown in front of his owner. You must stand still like a statue, don't say anything, don't move, and don't look at him.

Once the dog has calmed down, if he has not sat down on his own, ask him to sit. Once he is sitting, say "good" and pet him.

SITUATION AFTER EXTINCTION FOLLOWED BY REINFORCING GOOD BEHAVIOR: The dog thinks that to get attention he must sit calmly in front of his owner.

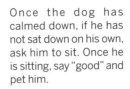

A Canine Role Model

This technique involves the dog learning through observation (see page 82) and reward (positive reinforcement). Your "student" dog will spend time with another dog—a role model—to modify his behavior using the role model's good behavior as an example. The role model must have mastered the behavior that you would like to modify in your own dog.

WHICH DOG SHOULD BE THE ROLE MODEL?

Your dog's mother or a canine friend that your dog is comfortable with, if well adjusted and well trained, can be an excellent role model. The role model is rewarded for good behavior in front of the student (in our example, the little girl rewards the role model dog who comes to say hello).

Through repetition, the student eventually adopts the behavior of the role model. This method is also used, in combination with other techniques, to overcome certain fears and to teach lessons, such as house-training and basic cues.

The role-model technique affirms all of the behavioral, social, and recreational benefits of a puppy learning in the company of well-adjusted dogs.

SITUATION: THE DOG IS AFRAID OF A LITTLE GIRL

SITUATION: The dog is afraid of a little girl and won't go anywhere near her.

This little girl is not someone I should trust.

The owner takes the dog for a walk with another dog, who likes the little girl because she is nice, pets him, and gives him treats. When the dog sees his friend approach the little girl with a wagging tail and watches the other dog receive petting and rewards, it reduces his apprehension.

My friend is not afraid of the little girl, and he gets attention and treats, so there is no reason not to be around her.

How Long Does Behavioral Change Take?

The speed of modifying a behavior depends on your dog, the behavior, and the environment. In any case, there is no miracle solution: patience and perseverance are essential.

CHANGE DOESN'T HAPPEN OVERNIGHT

No research has been conducted on dogs to determine the time required for behavioral change. As an indication, if we refer to an English study conducted on humans published in 2010 in the *European Journal of Social Psychology*, it takes an average of 66 days to adopt a new behavior, with extremes ranging from 18 to 254 days!

All of this is to make you understand that **change is never instantaneous.** Allow the process to take its course, repeat the exercises several times every day, and involve your family and friends in the process. Be patient, be forgiving, and don't get discouraged, and your dog will eventually achieve your objective. Above all, remember that when it comes to change, the clearer and more precise your goal is, the shorter the path will be to get there.

> If you know exactly what you want from your dog, you will find the resources to make it happen.

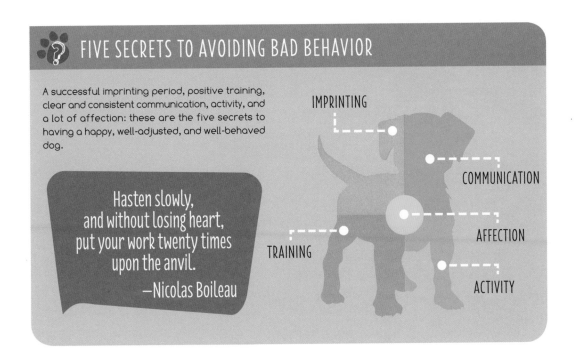

? FIVE SECRETS TO AVOIDING BAD BEHAVIOR

A successful imprinting period, positive training, clear and consistent communication, activity, and a lot of affection: these are the five secrets to having a happy, well-adjusted, and well-behaved dog.

> Hasten slowly, and without losing heart, put your work twenty times upon the anvil.
> —Nicolas Boileau

IMPRINTING

COMMUNICATION

AFFECTION

TRAINING

ACTIVITY

Summary of Techniques

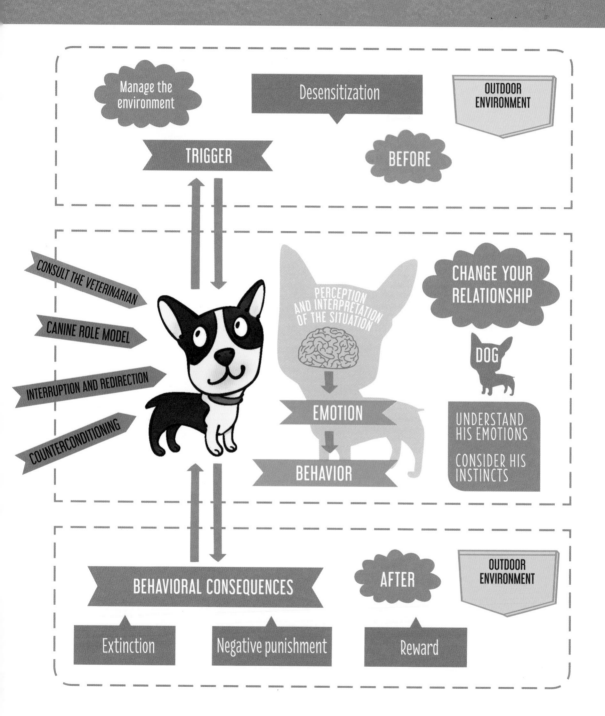

Manage the environment

Desensitization

OUTDOOR ENVIRONMENT

TRIGGER

BEFORE

CONSULT THE VETERINARIAN

CANINE ROLE MODEL

INTERRUPTION AND REDIRECTION

COUNTERCONDITIONING

PERCEPTION AND INTERPRETATION OF THE SITUATION

CHANGE YOUR RELATIONSHIP

DOG

EMOTION

UNDERSTAND HIS EMOTIONS

CONSIDER HIS INSTINCTS

BEHAVIOR

BEHAVIORAL CONSEQUENCES

AFTER

OUTDOOR ENVIRONMENT

Extinction

Negative punishment

Reward

THE MAIN CAUSES
OF UNWANTED BEHAVIOR

When Should Medications Be Used?

The use of medication is necessary when the dog's undesirable behavior is due to a physical (body-related) and/or psychological (brain-related) illness.

TREATING PHYSICAL ILLNESSES

Many undesirable behaviors can be caused by physical problems. In these cases, treatment is primarily medical, but sometimes also surgical.

OSTEOARTHRITIS, which is very common in older dogs, can lead to aggressive behavior or a state of depression due to chronic pain.
• **Treatment:** anti-inflammatory drugs, joint supplements, possibly surgery.

DIABETES, a metabolic disorder that leads to an increase in water intake and can cause urinary discomfort.
• **Treatment:** regular insulin injections, dietary changes, and weight management.

PANCREATIC INSUFFICIENCY, resulting in poor digestion and nutrient absorption, can cause chronic diarrhea and coprophagia (stool eating).
• **Treatment:** pancreatic enzyme replacement combined with supplementation and dietary changes.

HYPOTHYROIDISM can cause lethargy, irritability, anxiety, and even phobias.
• **Treatment:** thyroid hormone replacement.

CHRONIC RENAL FAILURE, frequent in older dogs, leads to an increase in water intake and can cause urinary discomfort, like diabetes.
• **Treatment:** dietary changes and medications to reduce the progression of disease.

BRAIN TUMORS can lead to sudden changes in behavior.
• **Treatment:** chemotherapy, radiation, surgery.

VISUAL IMPAIRMENT is often accompanied by an increase in fear reactions (aggression, flight, avoidance).

HEARING LOSS can lead to decreased attention, unwanted barking, and aggression.
• **Treatments for vison and hearing loss:** Depends on the origin of the impairment, but a decline in visual and auditory acuity is often irreversible in older animals.

TREATING PSYCHOLOGICAL ILLNESSES

Psychological illnesses can also lead to undesirable behaviors. They are treated with appropriate medications, nutraceuticals, and pheromones. The drugs act on neurotransmitters synthesized by neurons, among which the most common are dopamine, serotonin, and norepinephrine. Their use must be combined with behavior modification.

In the case of a phobia that causes behavioral manifestations of fear, reducing violent emotions through medical treatment is sometimes necessary for behavior modification.

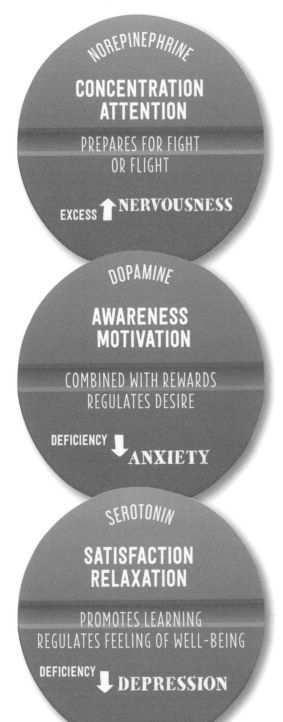

NOREPINEPHRINE

CONCENTRATION ATTENTION

PREPARES FOR FIGHT OR FLIGHT

EXCESS ↑ NERVOUSNESS

DOPAMINE

AWARENESS MOTIVATION

COMBINED WITH REWARDS REGULATES DESIRE

DEFICIENCY ↓ ANXIETY

SEROTONIN

SATISFACTION RELAXATION

PROMOTES LEARNING REGULATES FEELING OF WELL-BEING

DEFICIENCY ↓ DEPRESSION

BRAIN CHEMISTRY

Drugs prescribed by veterinarians to modify dogs' behavior act on the various neurotransmitters that regulate brain function. Certain drugs affect the central nervous system (CNS) and modify mental activity and behavior. These drugs act on the components of the CNS and on the neurotransmitters (e.g., norepinephrine, serotonin, dopamine) that transmit information throughout the CNS.

Clomipramine: At high doses, it improves sleep and reduces impulsiveness and aggression. At low doses, it treats anxiety and depression, promotes proper house-training, and allows the dog to be more independent. It increases the effects of norepinephrine and serotonin.

Selegiline is prescribed to treat phobias, anxiety, depression, and cognitive disorders in older dogs. It increases the effects of norepinephrine and dopamine.

Fluoxetine: At high doses, it regulates aggression, nervousness, and impulsiveness; at low doses, it treats anxiety and depression. It increases the effects of serotonin.

NUTRACEUTICALS

Nutraceuticals are made from compounds found in foods and have little risk of side effects, unlike drugs. Examples are Zylkene, based on a milk protein; Anxitane, based on amino acids found in green tea; and another that combines amino acids and vitamin B. They are used to reduce a dog's stress and fear in certain situations, such as being alone, hearing street noises or fireworks, traveling, and moving.

PHEROMONES

ADAPTIL® is an example of of a "dog appeasing pheromone"—a calming product based on pheromones secreted naturally by mother dogs after they give birth. It has a reassuring, soothing effect on puppies and reduces manifestations of stress induced by new experiences or situations. It is used in collars, diffusers, and sprays and is used to help dogs adapt to new environments (adoption, moving) and deal with stressful situations (such as the presence of street noises, fireworks, or storms).

CONCLUSION

THE BETTER YOU KNOW YOUR DOG, THE BETTER YOU CAN TRAIN HIM.

To train your dog well is not to train him to become what you want him to be, but to guide him to become what he can be by respecting his instincts and abilities. There are no "stupid" dogs—only dogs whose talents have not yet been developed by good owners.

If you dream of having a happy, loving, fulfilled, and well-behaved dog, be sure to invest understanding, time, patience, attention, and a big dose of love in his positive training, and you will recover your investment a hundredfold.

Benevolence is the best quality of a good trainer, and, as Mahatma Gandhi said, "The greatness of a nation and its moral progress can be judged by the way it treats animals."

YOUR DOG IS A TREASURE, AND YOU NOW KNOW HOW TO MAKE HIM SHINE.

ALL DOGS NEED POSITIVE TRAINING

Appendix

Timeline of Puppy Milestones 200
Training Timeline 202

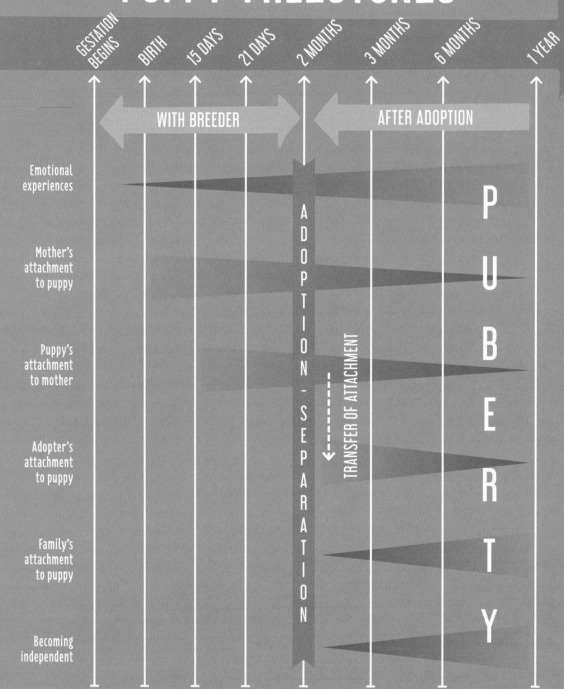

TIMELINE OF PUPPY MILESTONES

GESTATION BEGINS · BIRTH · 15 DAYS · 21 DAYS · 2 MONTHS · 3 MONTHS · 6 MONTHS · 1 YEAR

WITH BREEDER

AFTER ADOPTION

Emotional experiences

Mother's attachment to puppy

Puppy's attachment to mother

Adopter's attachment to puppy

Family's attachment to puppy

Becoming independent

ADOPTION - SEPARATION

TRANSFER OF ATTACHMENT

PUBERTY

TRAINING TIMELINE

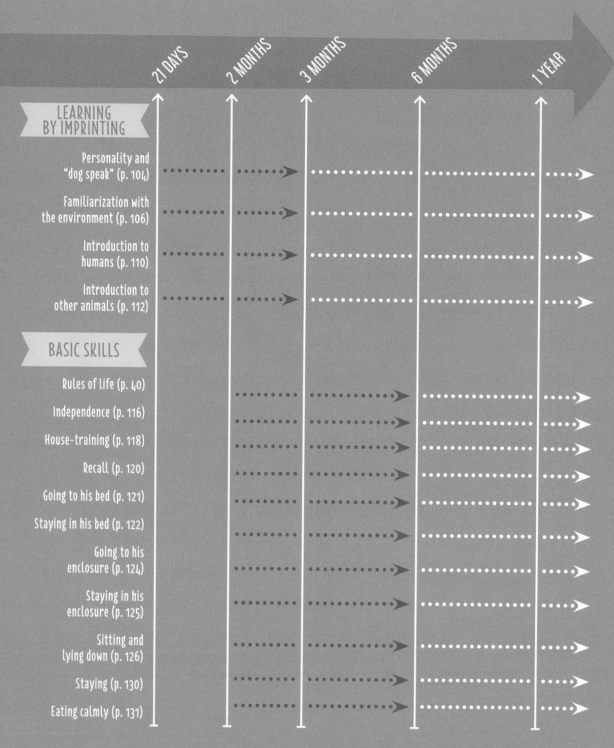

	21 DAYS	2 MONTHS	3 MONTHS	6 MONTHS	1 YEAR
LEARNING BY IMPRINTING					
Personality and "dog speak" (p. 104)	● ● ● ● ● ● ● ● ● ● ● ● →		● ●		● ● ● ● →
Familiarization with the environment (p. 106)	● ● ● ● ● ● ● ● ● ● ● ● →		● ●		● ● ● ● →
Introduction to humans (p. 110)	● ● ● ● ● ● ● ● ● →		● ●		● ● ● ● →
Introduction to other animals (p. 112)	● ● ● ● ● ● ● ● ● ● ● ● →		● ●		● ● ● ● →
BASIC SKILLS					
Rules of life (p. 40)		● ● ● ● ● ● ● ● ● ● ● ● ● ● ● ● ● ● →		● ● ● ● ● ● ● ● ● ● ● ● ● ● ● ● ● ● ● ●	→
Independence (p. 116)		● ● ● ● ● ● ● ● ● ● ● ● ● ● ● ● ● ● →		● ● ● ● ● ● ● ● ● ● ● ● ● ● ● ● ● ● ● ●	→
House-training (p. 118)		● ● ● ● ● ● ● ● ● ● ● ● ● ● ● ● ● ● →		● ● ● ● ● ● ● ● ● ● ● ● ● ● ● ● ● ● ● ●	→
Recall (p. 120)		● ● ● ● ● ● ● ● ● ● ● ● ● ● ● ● ● ● →		● ● ● ● ● ● ● ● ● ● ● ● ● ● ● ● ● ● ● ●	→
Going to his bed (p. 121)		● ● ● ● ● ● ● ● ● ● ● ● ● ● ● ● ● ● →		● ● ● ● ● ● ● ● ● ● ● ● ● ● ● ● ● ● ● ●	→
Staying in his bed (p. 122)		● ● ● ● ● ● ● ● ● ● ● ● ● ● ● ● ● ● →		● ● ● ● ● ● ● ● ● ● ● ● ● ● ● ● ● ● ● ●	→
Going to his enclosure (p. 124)		● ● ● ● ● ● ● ● ● ● ● ● ● ● ● ● ● ● →		● ● ● ● ● ● ● ● ● ● ● ● ● ● ● ● ● ● ● ●	→
Staying in his enclosure (p. 125)		● ● ● ● ● ● ● ● ● ● ● ● ● ● ● ● ● ● →		● ● ● ● ● ● ● ● ● ● ● ● ● ● ● ● ● ● ● ●	→
Sitting and lying down (p. 126)		● ● ● ● ● ● ● ● ● ● ● ● ● ● ● ● ● ● →		● ● ● ● ● ● ● ● ● ● ● ● ● ● ● ● ● ● ● ●	→
Staying (p. 130)		● ● ● ● ● ● ● ● ● ● ● ● ● ● ● ● ● ● →		● ● ● ● ● ● ● ● ● ● ● ● ● ● ● ● ● ● ● ●	→
Eating calmly (p. 131)		● ● ● ● ● ● ● ● ● ● ● ● ● ● ● ● ● ● →		● ● ● ● ● ● ● ● ● ● ● ● ● ● ● ● ● ● ● ●	→

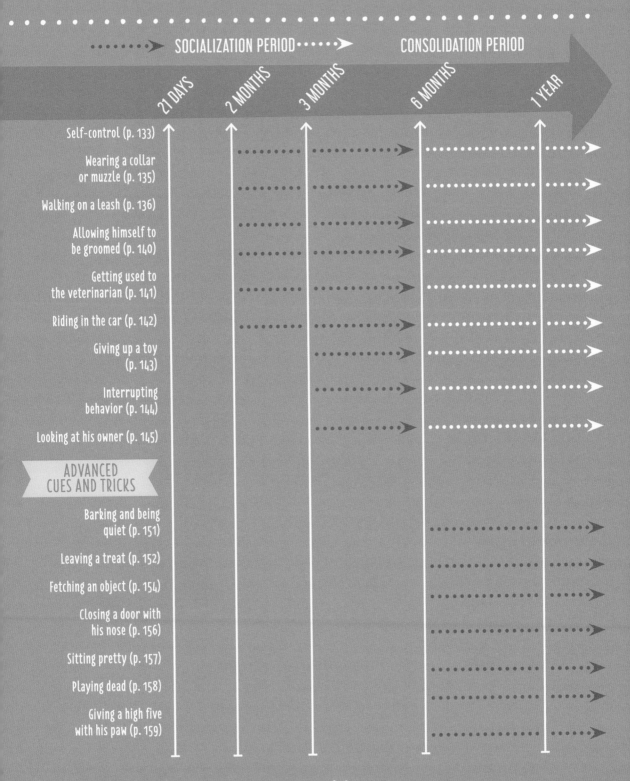

SOCIALIZATION PERIOD········➤   CONSOLIDATION PERIOD

21 DAYS   2 MONTHS   3 MONTHS   6 MONTHS   1 YEAR

Self-control (p. 133)

Wearing a collar
or muzzle (p. 135)

Walking on a leash (p. 136)

Allowing himself to
be groomed (p. 140)

Getting used to
the veterinarian (p. 141)

Riding in the car (p. 142)

Giving up a toy
(p. 143)

Interrupting
behavior (p. 144)

Looking at his owner (p. 145)

ADVANCED
CUES AND TRICKS

Barking and being
quiet (p. 151)

Leaving a treat (p. 152)

Fetching an object (p. 154)

Closing a door with
his nose (p. 156)

Sitting pretty (p. 157)

Playing dead (p. 158)

Giving a high five
with his paw (p. 159)

CAPTURING

A training method in which the trainer waits for the dog to spontaneously perform a desirable behavior and then reinforces the behavior with a reward and a verbal cue.

CONDITIONING

A mechanism for acquiring behaviors by combining two stimuli (classical conditioning) or establishing a link between a behavior and its consequences (operant conditioning). **Puppies start learning this way at a very early age. Conditioning is the basis of many training techniques but also of behavioral problems.**

Classical conditioning

The dog associates a stimulus from the environment with another stimulus, which elicits an automatic response from the dog: physiological (salivation, accelerated heart rate, sweating, chills, vomiting, bowel movements) and/or emotional (fear, excitement, joy). After training, the stimulus from the environment triggers the dog's automatic response. In this type of conditioning, the automated response is unintentional and beyond the dog's control.

Conventional conditioning results in what is called a *conditioned response*, because it is the stimulus that causes the response. The dog combines two stimuli and learns that one event predicts another. For example, if the owner gets the leash out every time he or she takes the dog for a walk, the dog will become excited each time his owner gets the leash.

Operant conditioning

The dog learns to associate a behavior with its consequences. If a behavior has pleasant consequences, its frequency tends to increase; conversely, if the consequences are unpleasant, the behavior tends to decrease.

In operant conditioning, the dog deliberately acts on his environment. He learns that his behavior has consequences. If, when his owner says "sit," the dog sits and receives a treat, he establishes an association between sitting when his owner says "sit" and receiving a treat (positive reinforcement). Thus, the probability that the dog will sit when his owner cues him to do so increases.

COUNTERCONDITIONING

A behavior modification technique consisting of combining a stimulus that triggers inappropriate behavior with a new, appropriate behavior that is incompatible with the inappropriate behavior. It is usually combined with desensitization.

DESENSITIZATION

A behavior modification technique resulting in the reduction of an inappropriate reaction to a stimulus by repeated exposure to the stimulus at gradually increasing intensity.

EXTINCTION

A behavior modification technique used to eliminate undesirable behavior by removing the elements that reinforce it.

LURING

A training method that consists of guiding the dog with a lure into the desired behavior. Food is the simplest and most practical lure because the dog will follow it closely with his nose.

NEGATIVE PUNISHMENT

A training method used to reduce the probability of undesirable behavior by removing something pleasant in response to the behavior.

NEGATIVE REINFORCEMENT

A training method that increases the probability of good behavior by removing something unpleasant in response to that behavior.

PHOBIA

An irrational and unjustified fear triggered by a particular situation.

POSITIVE PUNISHMENT

A training method that reduces the probability of undesirable behavior by introducing something unpleasant in response to that behavior.

POSITIVE REINFORCEMENT

A training method that increases the probability of good behavior by providing something pleasant in response to that behavior.

SHAPING

A method of training complex behavior by reinforcing successive approximations of the behavior.

INDEX

A

Advanced training, 146-159
Affection, 49
Agility (sport), 53
Anger, body language, 30
Anxiety, body language, 29-30
Avoidance, 79

B

Barking
- learning to, 151
- when the phone rings, 187
Barking, when the telephone
  rings, 187
Basic skills, 114-145
Bed, going to and staying in,
  121-122
Behavior modification, 162
- techniques, 178-192
Big dogs, fear of, 176-177, 186
Body language, 29-30
Bowls, choosing, 44
Breed groups, 18-19

C

Calmness, 131-132, 133-134, 139
Canicross, 53
Canine freestyle , 53
Capturing technique, 127
Car, riding in, 142
Chewing, 48
- desire to, 172
- electrical cords, 187
Children, fear of, 182, 191
Choosing a dog, 20-21, 55
Clicker training, 69, 84, 122,
  127, 129
Closing door with nose, 156
Collar, 84, 135
Come cue (Recall), 120
Communication
- with other dogs, 104-105
- types of, 32-37
Competitions, 53

Concentration, 27
Conditioning, 121
Counterconditioning, 183-186
Crouching, 29
Cues, communication of, 34-37

D

Dehydration, 43
Desensitization, 180-182,
  184-186
Diseases, 45
Domestication, 10-11
Drinking water, 42

E

Ears, position of, 29-30
Eating calmly, 131-132
Emotions
- considering, 172-173
- identifying, 28, 56
- understanding, 32
Enclosure, 84
- going into and staying in,
  124-125
Environment
- adaptation to, 106-107
- modification of, 169
Equipment, 84-85
Escape, 29, 79
Exercise pen, 84, 124-125
Extinction, 188-189
Eye contact with owner, 144

F

Facial expressions, 29-30, 36
False positive punishment, 73
Family, 41, 116, 166
Fear
- of big dogs, 176-177, 186
- of children, 182, 191
- posture, 29-30
- of trucks, 184
- of vacuum cleaner, 185
Feedback, cues, 35, 37

Fetching, 154-155
Food, 17, 43-44, 85
- refusal of, 30
Friends, 49
Frisbee, 53
Frustration, 134

G

Games, 52-53
Genome, 12, 14, 15
Gestation, 90
Greeting behavior, 133-134
Grooming, 140

H

Habituation, 106, 108
Hand signals, 36
Happiness, 56-57
-posture, 28
Harnesses, 135
Health, 44-45, 57, 141, 168,
  194-195
High Five cue, 159
House-training, 45, 118-119
Hugs, 93
Hunting behavior, 48
Hypervigilance, 30
Hypothermia, in puppy, 91

I

Identity, 104-105
Imprinting
- with adults, 110-111
- with animals, 112-113
- with children, 111
- period, 94-95
Independence, 116-117, 123
Instincts, 48
- considering the dog's,
  172-173
Interactions, 38-39
- absence of, 39
Interruption of
  behavior, 144, 187

J

Jackpot rewards, 68, 137
Jumping up for attention, 189

L

Learning by observation, 83
Leash walking, 85, 136-139
Licking lips, 29
Luring technique, 128
Lying down, 126-129

M

Massage, 50-51
Medication, use of, 194-195
Memory, 39
Mother's role in training, 16, 82
Muzzle, 135

N

Needs of dog, 42-54, 57
- basic, 42-43
- instinctive, 48
- physical activity, 52-53
- recreational, 49
- security, 46-47
- social, 49
- training, 54
- usefulness, 54
Negative punishment, 78
Neurons, 15
Nonverbal communication, 36

O

Observation, learning by, 83

P

Panting, 30
Paraverbal communication, 34
Perception of cues, 35
Pheromones, 196
- on collar, 117
Phobias, 108, 183
Physical activity, 52-53
Playing dead, 158
Playing, 49, 84
Positive punishment, 72-77
Postures (body language), 29-30

Q

Punishment, 63
- negative, 78
- positive, 72-77
Puppy classes, 105
Puppy development, 15-17
- first 15 days, 91, 92
- from 15 to 21 days, 92-93
- from 21 days to 2 months, 94-95
- from 2 to 6 months, 96-98, 100-101
- from 6 months to 1 year, 148

Quiet cue, 151

R

Recall (Come cue), 120
Redirecting behavior, 187
Refusal to give up toy, 174-175
Reinforcement, 63
- negative, 79
- positive, 64-67
Relationship, modification of, 170
Reproduction, 48
Rewards, 64-67
- effects of, 70-71
- efficacy of, 67
- jackpots, 68, 137
- secondary, 68
- unintentional, 70
Role model dog, 82-83, 190
Rules, establishing, 40-41

S

Sadness, posture, 31
Safety, 46-47
Schedule, 55, 56, 100, 150
Scratching, 30
Secondary punishment, 72
Secondary rewards, 68
Self-control, 131-132, 133-134, 139
Sensitization, 108
Shaking, 29
Shaping technique, 154
Sitting, 126-128
Sitting pretty, 157

Skills, 25

Skills, 25
Sleeping, 45
- in his bed, 121
Sniffing the ground, 30
Socialization, 103-113
"Speaking dog," 104-105
Staying alone, 122, 125
Stimuli, 106-107
Stop, 144
Street noises, desensitization to, 138
Stress, 57

T

Toy
- giving up, 143
- refusal to give up, 174-175
Training
- choice of method, 81
- need for, 54
- puppy, 17
- purpose of, 80
- trends, 62-63
Treat, leaving it, 152-153
Trucks, fear of, 184
Trust, relationship of, 38-39

U

Understanding cues, 34-35
Unintentional negative punishment, 78
Usefulness, 54

V

Vaccinations, 45
Vacuum cleaner, fear of, 185
Verbal communication, 34
Veterinarian, 44, 45, 141, 168

W

Wait cue, 130
Walking, 52, 105
- on a leash, 137-139
Wolves, 11

Y

Yawning, 30

Heartfelt thanks to
Véronique, Guillaume, Delphine, Céline, and Cyril
along with all of my dog friends, the source of my inspiration.

About the Author

Dr. Jean Cuvelier studied veterinary medicine at the National Veterinary School of Alfort in Maisons-Alfort, France, before starting a mobile veterinary practice available for in-home appointments 24 hours a day, 7 days a week. Every day, he visits all types of pets in their homes to provide them with care and educate their owners to foster harmony and happiness.

Dr. Cuvelier writes animal-related articles for many magazines, appears on radio and television programs, and is the author of numerous dog and cat books.

About the Illustrator

Jean-Yves Grall has been drawing since he was a child and has made a career out of his art through illustrations and graphic design, working in television, animation, book publishing, and corporate communications. Even though he's grown up, you can still find him with pencil in hand. He feels that the old adage about dogs and their owners resembling each other is often true, and he loves dogs because behind every great person is a faithful dog.

Illustrations bey Jean-Yves Grall except the following:
Infographics by Emmanuel Chaspoul: p. 14, 15 left, 28 top, 32, 34-35, 38 bottom, 39, 42 bottom, 56, 57, 60-61, 62, 63, 81, 88-89, 118 bottom, 150, 165, 170, 173, 178, 183 bottom, 191, 192, 195, 200, 202-203

Illustrations © Thinkstock p. 6, 28, 39, 44, 46 left, 47, 55

All photographs: © Thinkstock